DATE DUE

29 Nov '83	DEC 1 6 '95	
27 Dec '83	JAN 2 7 '96	
17 Dec '84		
30 Mar '85		
8 Apr '85		
NOV 1 8 '85		
DEC 2 6 '85		
OCT 14 '86		
APR 06 '87		
SEP 15 '87		
OCT 20 '87		
JUL 08 '88		
OCT 05 '91		
DEC 2 2 '91		
MAY 09 '92		
DEC 18 '92		
MAY 05 '94		
JAN 29 '95		
GAYLORD		PRINT

THE ALCOHOL TROUBLED PERSON:

Known
and
Unknown

THE ALCOHOL TROUBLED PERSON:

Known
and
Unknown

Alan Willoughby

Nelson-Hall Chicago

Willoughby, Alan.
   The alcohol troubled person.

   Includes index.
   1. Alcoholics—Rehabilitation—United States.
2. Alcoholics—United States—Family relationships.
I. Title.
HV5279.W54   362.2'92'0973   79-1173
ISBN 0-88229-426-1

Manufactured in the United States of America

10   9   8   7   6   5   4   3   2   1

*Most powerful is he who
has himself in his own power.*

Seneca

This work is dedicated to many people, but especially to:

My mother and father, Miranda G. and Raymond R. Willoughby, just because.

Ambrose Barry, M.D., an alcohol-damaged friend who beat it and died of its lasting consequences too few years later. A masterful Irish finagler, he would manipulate the Devil himself, or any other member of the Establishment, in the interests of a patient—especially an "alcoholic" one. I miss him.

William C. Redmon, M.D., whose wisdom and "frailties" have been so good for me as a person. We have learned to instruct one another, and he is the better instructor. He has even taught me, to the extent that I have learned it, to appreciate and to reward partial success, and his aphorisms are sprinkled throughout the book.

I have been fortunate indeed.

Contents

Introduction:
Encouragement and Hope

Above all else, this book is intended to provide hope and realistic encouragement to alcohol-damaged people, to their families, and to those who treat and help them. We have been shaped for too long by innumerable sayings and extremely deep-rooted beliefs that have the effect of unrealistically discouraging us. We know a great deal about positive approaches to alcohol problems, even though there is much to learn. New ideas and systems for locating and treating the problem have brightened the picture enormously.

We have a much higher success rate than we generally believe we have—far more alcohol-damaged people repair themselves quickly than slide into the stereotyped, chronic, "hopeless" state with which we are all familiar. Success occurs when accurate information is delivered quickly, simply, and unambivalently to the right person at the right time and when the information is imparted sensitively and in a way the person can understand.

Everyone knows an alcohol-damaged person or family, and almost everyone is able to recognize some such people when he sees them. The chronic losers, the extreme cases (and there are too many of them), are sometimes highly visible. But I've never been able to pick out the permanent loser ahead of time—or the big winner either. There are more of the latter, but, since they are actually just like the rest of us externally, we don't notice them after they've won.

If the wife of an alcohol troubled man is reading this book, perhaps it can rekindle some realistic hope in her. Or perhaps it can do the same for a college student whose mother is killing herself—or already has, or might start to some day. Or maybe it can offer hope to a parent with a twenty-year-old kid starting to go down the chute.

Accurate information and education are surprisingly powerful tools. In the area of alcohol troubles, however, it is sometimes difficult to get the right people first to *listen*, and then actually to *hear* and comprehend enough to change unhelpful attitudes and old wives' tales of misinformation. So this book is also written to try to fill some gaps in our practical knowledge and to dispel some of the counterproductive half-truths by which many people are governed in their behavior toward alcohol troubles.

In no other field that I know of can such miracles of positive change be worked so quickly for such huge numbers of people in trouble.

Sometimes it is necessary for the significant people involved in an alcohol problem to learn to place it in a paramount position in their lives for a time. Not forever, but for a while. If a person is in trouble with booze, it may be necessary for him or her to put the solution of that problem before considerations of embarrassment and pride, even before considerations of the distant future or present career, before children and spouse. Sometimes it seems that if the Four Horsemen of the Apocalypse—Conquest, War, Famine, and Death—were threatening, it would be necessary to continue resolutely in a straight line and remember that alcohol is, for the moment, more important.

If a father gives up on his alcohol-plagued son before making himself knowledgeable about the subject, he has certainly not put the problem in its proper perspective. If a wife is too socially embarrassed to speak to potential helpers of her troubled husband, she has not dealt with her own feelings.

There is no shame in having an alcohol problem oneself or having one in the family. Certainly, the alcohol troubled person is in a large enough group. The only *possible* shame is to have a problem and not deal with it.

There are many routes to help and many forms and sources of help. And they're getting impressively effective.

Another reason for writing this book is that I can't find any other one that says what I think needs to be said in a way that can be understood. I surely see bits and pieces here and there, but I don't see a book I can comfortably recommend to a class in "alcoholism" or a person in trouble.

I am even now sometimes troubled and, to tell the truth, angered and frustrated by the minds around me that are closed to new (or new to them, anyway) notions about this area. I believe that many people in the helping professions are literally criminally unaware with regard to alcohol problems. I include the surgeon who removes half a stomach rather than recognize an alcohol troubled person and either help him or refer him to where he can get help, and the psychologist who still thinks the swollen belly of a cirrhotic is a "tumor" and continues to treat for depression. I have met both of these professionals and many more like them.

I feel the same way about nonprofessionals who gain restricted knowledge about alcohol problems through their own experiences and act as if that's all there is to know.

From my current perspective in the academic world, I am sure that we can increase the number of educators who know about alcohol issues and who can become willing and able to help. Sometimes I feel that I am in a nest of "educated idiots," and sometimes I am awed by the abilities of my colleagues, but mostly I know they're simply not informed but mean well and *think* they are informed.

In addition, I always feel a discomfort with people in public policy-making positions in areas concerning alcohol who do not actually work with clients at least part of the time and who as a result hammer out policy that leads down dead-end paths. This happens at federal, state, and local levels. Still, we have made tremendous progress in just the last few years despite the aforementioned drawbacks.

I hope this effort will help at least a little.

The book is longer and more complicated than it was meant to be. I struggle with how much is left out, yet I wanted to produce a practical handbook, a usable guide for the home, office, and classroom—something that real people can read. I would be proud to hear that some copies have been read on the hopper, where some of our greatest minds are at work.

I am genuinely encouraged by the advances in attitude and the increased effectiveness of treatment, and hope that you can share that encouragement with me as you read.

1
Why Would Anyone Drink Like That Anyway?

Only that day dawns to which we are awake.
Henry David Thoreau

Alcohol has attained magical properties in our society. We have "happy hours." Alcohol is "good for what ails you" and is a "pick-me-up"; it puts hair on your chest, cures coughs and colds, and staves off pneumonia; it is widely used as an aphrodisiac ("Give her a couple of beers and afterward she can blame it on that"); and it is regularly used to express feelings of celebration, sadness, and anger. It is invested with powerful symbolic and religious meaning—it can variously signify the blood of Christ, the attainment of puberty or adulthood, masculinity, sophistication, good fellowship, trust, despair, or joy. You drink a toast at important affairs of state or to wish other people well—sometimes you smash your glass against the fireplace if you're a member of the "old-school tie" or Bengal Lancers bunch, or you crunch it under your heel if you're at a Jewish wedding.

Champagne is likely to symbolize one set of feelings; beer has another connotation; "good scotch" another. Wine can be genteel, or romantic (when accompanied by either a

1

candle or a loaf of bread and thou), or the last resort when
you've sunk so low you can't afford anything else. Prestige
and packaging also seem to make a difference; the connois-
seur generally (not always but generally) thinks he has a
great drink if you put rotgut in a high-class bottle, but he
hates the drink if you put "good stuff" in a rotgut bottle.

The recent Bordeaux wine scandal in France made the
point well. The French government, which protects and
supervises the labeling of wines, uncovered a long-term successful plot to substitute cheap wines for "good" Bordeaux.
Some bottles were apparently labeled without altering their
contents, while the wine in others was altered by the addition of chemicals. Professional tasters could not tell the
difference. Imagine the number of people who had sniffed
the "bouquet" of the cheap wines while expounding on the
incomparable virtues of Bordeaux '33!

The packagers of imported country wines go to great
lengths to maintain a pastoral atmosphere in their adver-
tising; yet an internationally known winery in Portugal
ships its grape juice from a hundred miles away in gigantic
tank trucks, mixes it in stainless steel and ceramic vats,
complete with modern valves and plumbing, carbonates it
just as one would a soft drink, and packages it on an assembly line—in simulated earthenware crocks. (At least it's
clean. In Madeira the operation of pouring wine off the
sludge in the bottom of the cask is performed in a muddy,
dirty open shed. As it is poured, the wine runs down the side
of the ancient, dirty, definitely-touched-by-human-hands
barrel into the next cask.)

In addition to being lured by magic and prestige, what
other reasons do people have for drinking? There are many,
of course, but primary among them is the fact that man's
state of consciousness is altered by the chemical alcohol.
Clearly, not all people have trouble with alcohol, and many
use it, regularly or irregularly, without any harm whatever
and in a responsible fashion that modestly increases that
pleasure in their lives.

I take no abolitionist point of view; my argument throughout is simply that if one gets into trouble with alcohol it pays to notice the fact and do something constructive about it.

I am not primarily concerned with the amount of alcohol consumed or with whether people become "alcoholics" in the usually understood sense of the term, but only with whether or not the use of the chemical produces significant trouble or pain. Sometimes, of course, in practical clinical cases such issues must be addressed, but in general the situation can be handled better if we concern ourselves with the *problems*, not with the amount or the form of the chemical.

Some Reasons Commonly Given for Drinking

The specific reasons for drinking alcohol that are dealt with here can help us to see that a variety of reasons are used to "explain" the widespread use of alcohol. It is common for people to drift into troubled drinking via one of these routes; once in trouble, the individual should not use these reasons to explain and support continued destructive use of alcohol. Thus, social custom may lead one into drinking behavior which hurts one. Once in trouble, a person cannot use social custom as a reason for continued, uninformed, counterproductive behavior.

Social Custom and Social Lubricant

Since alcohol reduces inhibition and serves in the short run as a reducer of anxiety, particularly the anxiety generated by social stress, it is widely used in social settings; these are sometimes called cocktail parties. The effects of alcohol permit many people to interact more comfortably with others than they could otherwise—not a bad thing at all. Men become more handsome and women more lovely, and everyone becomes more intelligent, witty, and acceptable—to themselves, at any rate. Good fellowship, warmth, and a decrease in loneliness *do* occur in these settings, and one can sometimes feel a bit uncomfortable arriving at a cocktail party two drinks late. That problem is readily solved, of course.

As we will see, subcultural group pressures and norms with regard to alcohol are part of the pervasive social customs under which we all live.

Anesthetic Properties

The analgesic or anesthetic properties of alcohol are well known, and its use as a painkiller sometimes seems almost legitimate. Usually, however, it is far better to obtain an appropriate prescription, because in the long run or in an alcohol troubled person this particular chemical is counterproductive as a painkiller. In this day and age we dig out very few bullets in the corral without anesthetics.

Taste

Many people enjoy the taste of the drinks in which their alcohol is carried. Beer is enjoyed by many, and it always amazes me how many people actually like martinis and manhattans and drink them for that reason as well as for the chemical effect. Despite desperate efforts in my younger days, I could never acquire a taste for those two myself—my preference has been for sweeter, smoother drinks.

Often, taste gets confused with conviviality in people's minds, but there is no question that some people like the flavor of a particular alcoholic drink.

It is important to state that (1) significant numbers of people in serious trouble with alcohol have never acquired a liking for the taste but instead drink for the effect *despite* the taste, and (2) continued drinking in an alcohol troubled individual for taste reasons cannot be considered legitimate.

Soporific Properties

Sleep disturbances are not uncommon in our society, and various medications and chemicals—"sleepers"—are available to handle these problems. They run the gamut from over-the-counter drugs, through prescription drugs, to alcohol, which is probably the most widely used of all.

Sleep disturbances sometimes accompany physical problems or medical syndromes, but the vast majority are caused by psychic, or emotional, factors. Depression and/or anxiety are by far the most common culprits, and people suffering those vastly uncomfortable and often desperate states feel so nearly unable to bear an ounce more pain that they begin to take chemicals of various sorts. Most of us have had nights like that. For many, the obsessive ruminations, the nonstop turnover of thoughts through a hatefully active brain is terribly hard to bear. One can empathize with the individual whose life is going sour and who can't face having one more thing go wrong. Yet the fact is that except in severe clinical cases of psychic distress the human machinery will run until it has to rest, and then it will rest. People often complain that they are "not sleeping a wink," but a close examination discloses that the person is getting four to six hours of sleep in twenty-four when he or she believes that seven or nine is necessary. Typically, the machinery functions nicely and efficiently on four hours or so for an amazing length of time even in those who are most comfortable with ten hours' sleep.

Alcohol helps some such people sleep over the short haul, as do the almost equally dangerous relatives, the barbiturates. Alcohol and barbiturates tend, frighteningly, to get combined, and both actually lead over long and heavy usage to an increase in jitteriness, a lessened overall ability to sleep without them, and an increase in tolerance (a gradual buildup of a kind of immunity so that the body needs more to produce a given effect).

This discussion of sleep disturbances does not deal with

the sleeplessness and overreactivity of the nervous system when *withdrawing* from alcohol and barbiturates after addiction has occurred. *That* kind of sleepless jitteriness can lead to grave consequences discussed later. Suffice it to say now that persons helping an alcohol troubled person should be aware of the extent of physiological addiction before undertaking or urging medically unsupported withdrawal— it can be dangerous indeed, even fatal.

People do *not* drink destructively because of allergy, heredity, or because they were born that way, contrary to opinions widely held in some circles.

Tranquilizing Properties

Despite the manifold theories explaining why people drink, one absolutely inescapable fact underlies every drinking problem and requires attention in each one:

Alcohol is, purely and simply, an efficient tranquilizer or short-term anxiety reducer, although there are critical drawbacks dictating that it be used for this purpose only with extreme care.

At rock bottom, the primary reason man over the ages has fermented various materials into ethyl alcohol has been to reduce the unpleasant feelings of fear and anxiety that all of us occasionally or frequently experience. We run less scared and inhibited for a while after we take this feel-better drug.

Our wide usage of alcohol is so taken for granted that it is hard to get a perspective on it. The idea of taking a pill to make life seem happier and more worth living seemed Buck Rogerish fifteen years ago. Now we use and abuse such pills regularly and call them tranquilizers. Many adults remain wary of marijuana even though it is clearly not as addicting as their own tranquilizer, alcohol. This is not an ad or plug for pot—some people can't handle it and get into trouble with it and others get demotivated for awhile, but at least they don't destroy their livers or die in withdrawal.

I am amused by the pharmacology professor, or the local minister, or whoever who flits from one seminar and high school to another denigrating the use of pot and "hard drugs" without mentioning the problem of alcohol—the "hardest" drug around. These "experts" often say that if you smoke pot you will probably end up on heroin, since marijuana is found in the background of "every" heroin user.

This argument depends, however, on which direction you face—forward or backward. It is true that if you look backward in the life of an addictive heroin user you will usually find a history of marijuana, along with nicotine, alcohol, and several other consciousness-altering chemicals. Persons with addictive personalities are known to use chemicals of many varieties to feel different. If one carries this "logic" to its limits, one may find that each heroin addict also once used mother's milk and Gerber's baby foods. A causal relationship is not thereby established.

Looking forward, however, one cannot predict that a pot user will become a heroin addict—most do not, although clearly the greater the usage of feeling-altering chemicals the greater the likelihood that the user is at high risk for some kind of chemical abuse. People around colleges and universities suspect that the top quarter of the students— the creative, socially aware, gifted kids—are often on pot. The bottom quarter—dull, unmotivated, and unproductive —also tend to use it heavily.

APPARENT ADVANTAGES OF ALCOHOL

Several factors conspire to produce widespread use of alcohol as a mind-and-consciousness-alterer and reducer of anxiety:

1. *Alcohol is almost universally effective.* It works for practically everybody. This fact is not true of prescription tranquilizers, the dosage of which the physician may have to manipulate for a time before optimal effect is achieved. Tranquilizers may have to be prescribed in

combination with another drug, depending on the effect on the individual, or the physician may have to try several drugs before the best one is found.

2. *The best dosage is easy to figure out by yourself.* Sometimes if you're tired, upset, or hungry when you start drinking, the alcohol will have an atypical effect, and punch is pretty hard to predict sometimes, but most of us know what two beers or three martinis will ordinarily do to us.

   After a little practice, usually in the late teens, you can not only figure out the best tension-reducing total volume, but also readily become sophisticated enough to regulate the speed with which you take successive drinks. If you are late to a cocktail party, you simply get two quick ones in. You discover that according to your mood and intent it's best either to take it slow and build up to a nice mellow good feeling, or to slug a few down quickly to get up high and coast. Each of us develops different patterns and prior intents, and most can gauge the dose pretty accurately.

   Interestingly enough, this ability to control dosage is true even of such people as the patrons of big-city "morning bars." These individuals are pretty involved in alcohol; they are severe cases who can't get by the morning shakes and get off to work without a few stiff jolts. But they know how many will reduce the tremulousness and permit them to get through the day.

3. *Alcohol works quickly as a tension-reducer.* Again, in contrast to the mode of action of prescription drugs, the effects of alcohol are almost immediate for most people —within two to five minutes—and we learn quickly either to drink more rapidly or to consume a more concentrated form in order to feel the drug faster.

   Contrast alcohol with the antidepressant prescription medication (a stupendously useful boon to mankind) that must build up in the bloodstream over an average of seven to fourteen days for effectiveness. Or

Thorazine by mouth, which averages 1½ to eight hours, or Librium, which requires ½ to 1½ hours. And remember, they don't always work and booze does!

4. *Alcohol is readily available.* It's everywhere and requires no prescription. You needn't go through all that bother of visiting a physician and running the risk of having him minimize your psychic discomfort or tell you to toughen up or straighten out or stop feeling sorry for yourself. To take a drink of booze doesn't even require the awareness that you're taking nerve medicine. After all, everyone drinks now and again to let down and relax. You can get alcohol without much delay or inconvenience.

5. *It's socially acceptable.* I'd like to have a nickel for every woman I've seen who secretly or not-so-secretly felt her friends on tranquilizers were self-indulgent or weak or without character until her turn came for anxiety episodes. Then she says, "Oh, wow! Now I know what Marie went through."

But until it's overdone, and often even then, society accepts alcohol. "I can understand George drinking lately. With a job (kid, yard, automobile, father, wife, outlook, history, toothache) like that, who wouldn't?"

Readers who have overcome or are overcoming alcohol troubles will testify to the large numbers of people who in fact act resentful when alcohol troubled people try to cut back. Recovering "alcoholics" learn to sniff their nonalcoholic beverages at parties or have their spouses test them to foil the "friend" who spikes drinks.

Drinking is nothing if not socially acceptable.

6. *It's cheap.* If you go to your physician to get a prescription it will cost you at least ten dollars, even if he doesn't request X-rays and lab work. Alcohol will cost you fifty cents to a dollar for an anxiety-reducing dose. It's cheap per unit of tension reduction.

With all these advantages, it is not surprising that large numbers of people use alcohol, sometimes in considerable quantity. And my position is that there is nothing inherently bad about alcohol *unless it causes trouble* (although there is nothing particularly wonderful about it either).You won't find me taking a teetotaler stand.

Disadvantages of Alcohol

On the other hand, the facts force me to present and give at least equal time to the potential dangers of the use of this particular chemical.

Interestingly, you can begin to list disadvantages simply by enumerating the advantages: effective, self-prescribed, fast-acting, readily available, socially acceptable, and cheap. If you link these characteristics with a substance that presents a potentially explosive danger—which you can very easily—the situation is analogous to handing out loaded shotguns. Some dummies would blow their own heads off; others would blast down every tree in sight; some nonvegetarians would catch their dinners efficiently; some would solve their marital problems. The fact that not everyone would use his or her shotgun appropriately (whatever that might mean with a shotgun) is not the main reason to eliminate them. One needs instead to inform and train people about their use.

In short, *all the advantages of alcohol usage as an anxiety reducer are easily transformed into very dangerous characteristics in the wrong hands.*

Addictive Properties

Alcohol is a highly addicting and addictive drug; heroin is no more addicting. Just as with alcohol, it is possible for some people to use heroin without getting caught by it.

Here we need to make a distinction between the terms *psychological dependency* and *physiological addiction.* The person who feels underprotected and restive without a drug, who feels as if he or she can't function well or comfortably without it, depends on it *psychologically*.

I once had some tough dental work done, and I had no way of predicting when a wave of excruciating pain might engulf me. I began carrying aspirin as well as a stronger painkiller with me wherever I went, and the temporary upshot of these circumstances was a psychological dependence. I was, in fact, highly anxious—scared to death—if I happened to go anywhere without my protecting medication. I might have used only one pill every third or eighth day, but I was jittery without them near me.

Psychological dependence can be powerful. My mother-in-law, now in her seventies, is psychologically dependent on beer and apples. She can't sleep if she doesn't have an apple and eight ounces of beer at night. She never consumes any more of either—she's never been known to have two apples or nine ounces of beer—and she's been doing this for over fifty years. She worries herself into a genuinely uncomfortable state if she doesn't follow her ritual.

Physiological addiction is quite another thing and can be recognized by the presence of two characteristics—the buildup of tolerance and/or the occurrence of withdrawal symptoms when the chemical is no longer taken.

Tolerance to a chemical may build up as one uses it—one then needs to use more of the drug to get the same effect that was earlier produced by less. Dexedrine used to be prescribed to get people started in the morning if they were depressed—since the tolerance level built up steadily, anyone who took increasing amounts of the medication might suddenly collapse or run a car into a tree.

Withdrawal symptoms in alcohol addiction can be desperate indeed—physical effects include shakes and tremulousness, perspiration, fear and suspiciousness, epileptic seizures, delirium tremens (DTs or pink elephants), anger episodes and rages, coma, and other severe physical changes as the body readjusts to absence of the drug. It is not widely known, but withdrawing from alcohol is infinitely more difficult, painful, and dangerous than coming off heroin. The latter is like having an uncomfortable case of the flu— aching, congested nasal passages and runny nose, knowing damned well you'd feel better if you had some more of the junk that got you in this fix in the first place.

People don't die in heroin withdrawal. They do in alcohol withdrawal—in a "rum fit" (an alcohol-induced seizure); in DTs; from dehydration, malnutrition, heart failure, exhaustion.

Alcohol is a "hard drug." It is readily addicting physiologically and also readily generates psychological dependency. It is as addicting as or more so than barbiturates and the opium derivatives. Like them, it hooks some and lets others off.

I write this in Rhode Island, which has a population of about a million. We have here a minimum of 40,000 *hardcore*, chronic, severely damaged alcohol addicts. This number does not include moderately damaged individuals, and it is my personal conviction that if we could agree on definitions of the problem we would have a higher number. We have a *maximum* of 600 hard-core opium-derivative addicts. The ratio of 40,000 (minimum) alcohol-damaged to 600 (maximum) "hard-drug" slaves is 66 to 1. In alcohol work we get upset when we hear experts speak of "drugs or alcohol." We say "alcohol and other drugs."

So one disadvantage of using alcohol to reduce anxiety is that it is unarguably addicting—not to all, but to plenty of people.

Alcohol can be subtle and silent in gaining its grip. In wide and social use, usually building tolerance, addiction, and dependency slowly, alcohol often has been revealed to be a problem in people who were not aware of the problem until five or ten or twenty years after they had it!

The use of alcohol to decrease depression and/or anxiety increases the severity of the original problem. Over a short period it works fairly well for most, because after all it *does* have all the advantages just noted.

Over the long haul (two months or more, sometimes less) alcohol burdens the depressed user with increased depression and increases anxiety in the person who drinks to overcome short-term tension.

It is necessary here to introduce the concept of 72 to 96 hours, which keeps cropping up in alcohol work.

Antabuse, a medication an alcohol troubled person can take to protect himself against casual or thoughtless drinking, is generally effective for about 72 to 96 hours (three to four days). During this period, it makes the person who uses it sick if he drinks.

If a depressed person drinks on a Friday, the result will be a subtle but significant rise in depression even until Monday or Tuesday, or, again, 72 to 96 hours.

People at risk for delirium tremens (those who have been chronically and heavily imbibing, usually without proper nutrition, and who then reduce or stop drinking) are vulnerable for 72 to 96 hours after reduction or cessation of alcohol consumption.

Anxiety level and neural overreactivity decrease significantly for one to three hours or so after a drink, then increase, subtly and *cumulatively*, one increment on top of the other, for the familiar three to four days.

I am indebted to Dr. Stanley Gitlow for the following concept and manner of presenting these facts—I have used this format for myself and others since I heard him use it at a seminar, and have changed it only slightly. It makes good sense.

The graphs presented here are set up to show at the zero point a condition of no anxiety, which is of course only fleetingly possible in the human condition. The first graph depicts the level of anxiety or tension as it might be in an average person. It has, of course, ups and downs. The second graph depicts the situation for an alcohol-involved individual.

Although my psychologist colleagues may accuse me of oversimplifying, I will for present purposes call anxiety or tension a physiological state characterized by discomfort and edginess. The condition is often attributable to emo-

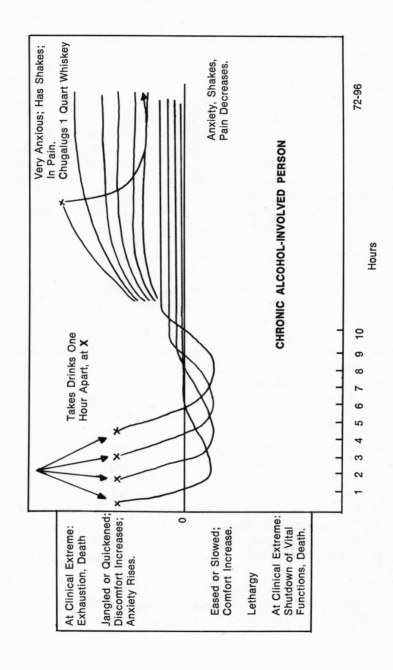

14

Very Anxious; Has Shakes;
In Pain.
Chugalugs 1 Quart Whiskey

Anxiety, Shakes,
Pain Decreases.

Takes Drinks One
Hour Apart, at **X**

At Clinical Extreme:
Exhaustion, Death

Jangled or Quickened;
Discomfort Increases;
Anxiety Rises.

0

Eased or Slowed;
Comfort Increase.

Lethargy

At Clinical Extreme:
Shutdown of Vital
Functions, Death.

1 2 3 4 5 6 7 8 9 10

Hours

72-96

CHRONIC ALCOHOL-INVOLVED PERSON

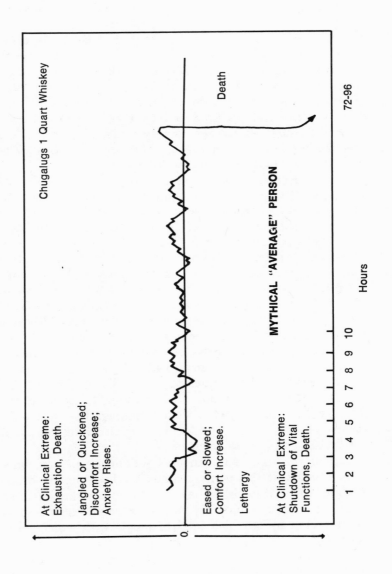

Chugalugs 1 Quart Whiskey

At Clinical Extreme: Exhaustion, Death.

Jangled or Quickened; Discomfort Increase; Anxiety Rises.

0

Eased or Slowed; Comfort Increase.

Lethargy

At Clinical Extreme: Shutdown of Vital Functions, Death.

Death

MYTHICAL "AVERAGE" PERSON

1 2 3 4 5 6 7 8 9 10

Hours

72-96

15

tional or situational circumstances, but it is in any event accompanied by physical change—increase in heartbeat; increase of the (electrical) galvanic skin response; sudden drops or, more usually, rises in blood pressure; overreactivity to stimuli (slam a door near a nervous person); and the like. The feelings produced by these changes are expressed in such phrases as "jittery," "jangled nerves," "I feel like jumping out of my skin," "The top of my head feels as if it would blow off," and so forth.

A dip in the graphs indicates a reduction in this internal physical activity that man regularly declines to tolerate, and a rise shows an increase in undesirable stimuli. In the latter case the machinery is firing at an uncomfortable rate.

The important factor to be noted in the graphs is that a drink of alcohol reduces the "jangle," but then it subsequently increases. The drink wears off quickly (one to three hours), but the slight "jangling" effect persists for three to four days, so that in the second graph the alcohol-damaged individual is unbearably anxious after prolonged drinking and is firing rapidly on all neurological cylinders.

If the person unaccustomed to consuming quantities of alcohol were to drink a quart, or sometimes even a pint, of whiskey very quickly (chugalug) he or she might well die, since the firing level is relatively low and no tolerance to the drug has been built up by regular drinking. Teen-agers kill themselves this way by accident. The breathing center of the brain simply shuts down.

If, on the other hand, an alcohol-damaged person chugalugs a quart at this point, his anxiety level merely drops to about where it ought to be—the slowing, easing effect so drastically entered into his computer counteracts and is counteracted by the high level of jangle with which he is burdened.

The point of the graphs is not, of course, to demonstrate that it is safe for the alcohol-damaged person to drink and unsafe for others. Rather, the graphs demonstrate what we see in clinical practice—a highly traumatic, difficult, and often dangerous descent to a nondrinking state for the actively drinking, damaged person. The distance he sometimes has to travel, and the distress he may have to live through, is dramatically underscored by the fact that he is *so* entangled that a dose that would be literally lethal for anyone else just straightens him out—temporarily. Be it remembered, however, that 72 to 96 hours after the chugalug quart he'll again have to face the music, only still worse.

To summarize, each of the advantages of alcohol can quickly become dangerous for some people. In addition, alcohol is an addictive drug that is subtle and insidious. In the long run it increases anxiety and depression, the very states it is paradoxically used to decrease. A final major disadvantage is really a four-part disadvantage—alcohol troubles are defined as being present if the financial, social, emotional, and/or physical areas of life are adversely affected. These definitional matters are important enough to deserve a chapter, so their discussion will be reserved for Chapter 4.

Alcohol Consumption: A Learned Response

As mentioned earlier, despite several peripheral causes for drinking, in the last analysis alcohol is used to control uncomfortable or unbearable feelings of dis-ease.

In this regard I refer to a very simple diagram that symbolizes and to some extent helps describe a popular, useful, and sometimes complicated system called *learning theory*:

$$S-R_x$$

S = Stimulus or stimulation, from either outside or inside the person.

$-$ = Habit, or learning bond, or learning.

R = Response, or action, on the part of the person.

x = Reinforcement, or payoff, or reward.

If an individual feels a stimulus called anxiety and for one reason or another performs the action of drinking alcohol, and if that action leads to the *quick* reduction of the immediate anxiety (as it will, we have seen), then the line between the *S* and the *R* will be strengthened. This means that if the same individual feels that same kind of anxiety again (discomfort in a group of people, for example) the likelihood that he will again make the response of taking a drink is increased—he got a quick payoff the first time, didn't he? If the response to the anxiety is again paid off with a quick reduction in tension, the learning is increased some more.

Learning is sometimes a lot more complex than it looks. For example, we make these connections all the time without even knowing it. Sometimes we learn better (or at least the learning lasts longer) if we don't get rewarded every time. (How can you give up a costly betting habit right away if you hit it big every once in a while?)

And how exactly do you define a quick payoff? And will a large reward later sometimes hasten learning better than a little one right away?

I once knew a man who was severely and chronically damaged by alcohol. At least a part of him wanted to quit and yet he kept drinking, without registering it until too late, so he tried Antabuse, the medication that makes you sick in combination with alcohol. He was brought into the hospital in a severe Antabuse reaction—he had learned so well and so unconsciously that booze produced a quick reduction of tension that he had gulped a half pint of whiskey, somehow foggily aware that he should hurry to get his payoff before the Antabuse reaction hit.

The principle of quick reward is strong. People who have a solid S-R bond regarding alcohol regularly trade the quick payoff for a later ulcer, or a later night in the cold rain, or later shame and guilt, or later loss of husband or wife and family.

We will talk about ways to break up the bond between

alcohol and anxiety reduction later. The point here, however, is that people *learn* to drink in a way that becomes destructive. They can also learn better ways to handle their feelings and fears. Some learn surprisingly quickly, some with agonizing slowness, and some, to be honest, not at all. Alcohol consumption is *not genetic*. Since it is learned, it can be unlearned or relearned.

2
Myths
and Misinformation

Just a Drink or Two

If you absolutely cannot refrain from drinking, start a saloon in your own home. Be the only customer, and you will not have to buy a license. Give your wife $18 to buy a gallon of whiskey. There are 128 snorts in a gallon. Buy all your drinks from your wife at a dollar and in four days—when the gallon is gone—your wife will have $110 to put in the bank and $18 to buy another gallon. If you live 10 years and buy all your booze from your wife and then die with snakes in your boots, she will have $108,774.34 on deposit—enough to bury you respectably, bring up the children, buy a house and lot, marry a decent man and forget she ever knew you.

Author Unknown
(With apologies to the author for
updating in terms of today's prices)

Alcohol has spawned a fantastic number of myths and a great deal of misinformation. We need an infusion of common sense. Some of the major fairy tales will be discussed in this chapter; others are inserted in the narrative elsewhere.

Some myths require special attention because they are widespread and tend to determine attitudes, or because they are particularly damaging to efforts at improving the situation, or both.

Myth I:
The Necessity of Psychotherapy

The first myth regarding alcohol goes thus: "Since the problem of alcoholism flows from psychological maladjustment, the only way to change the alcoholism is to go into some form of counseling or psychotherapy." The mythological rationale continues: "After the stresses that caused the problem drinking are reduced, the alcohol problem will either go away or can be addressed directly."

Most professionals believe Myth I. Such a widespread, incorrect belief is terribly damaging to efforts at grappling with alcohol problems. It drives alcohol-wise helping persons (usually recovered alcoholics) away from professionals as a class. The only fact that recommends its continuing existence is that it permits us to identify with great certainty and rapidity those professionals who believe themselves to be competent in the area but are not.

The rebuttal to Myth I is very simple. The individual in trouble with alcohol is functioning with a brain that either does not work or is working as if it were damaged, which in fact it is. One cannot talk to, and be heard by, a broken, crazy brain. The subtle nuances and delicate semantics indulged in by therapists who believe Myth I are largely forgotten, distorted, misunderstood, and in general not attended to by the recipient. The alcohol troubled person, whether intoxicated or not, often suffers from "blackouts" that prevent him from recalling periods and episodes in his life for sometimes a day or two. He is, even without blackouts, unable to attend with balance and stability to events in his environment and within himself. He may be extremely irritable, suspicious, tremulous; he is probably attending to the discomforts of his body, such as bellyaches or traumatic injuries; he is quite likely to be depressed and to be indulging in "stinking thinking," which is poor judgment coupled with overreaction or underreaction to important aspects of his life. His brain may in fact be toxic, or poisoned, and the rest of his body may not be functioning properly.

When the liver is cirrhotic, it cannot completely metabolize proteins, and the excess of intermediate products in the bloodstream can cause confusion, hallucinations, and schizophrenic-like attitudes and perceptions, and can lead to hepatic coma and even death. In other words, a cirrhotic is pumping through his brain blood that does not have the proper chemicals for normal, constructive functioning. It is as if he were looking into a distorted mirror (the perceptions being chemically distorted). Under such circumstances we must expect the person to perceive and respond in an irrational way.

Additionally, the alcohol-involved person is responding to other uncomfortable, frightening physical changes, which may in fact be excruciating. He also suffers from a multitude of psychological ills, including but not confined to depression, guilt, fear, and anxiety.

The answer to Myth I, then, is that you cannot make sense or establish a memory bank from which withdrawals can be made at appropriate times and in rational ways if you are dealing with a broken brain. Paradoxically, you must stop or significantly reduce the drinking before you can treat the alcohol problem.

Myth II:
Talking with an Intoxicated Person Is Helpful

Professionals often spend considerable amounts of time talking to patients or clients who are intoxicated. Myth II states that this is profitable. It is noted repeatedly in this book that intoxication does not necessarily identify the alcohol troubled person. Even our discussion of Myth I, for example, does not depend entirely on the existence of an intoxicated state. On the other hand, practical experience has demonstrated that almost the only thing to do with the intoxicated individual is to help him become detoxified, so that the next time you deal with him you can deal with a brain that is less broken. If a counselor, psychotherapist, physician, psychiatrist, psychologist, nurse, or any other professional regularly attempts to talk in a supposedly helpful way with an intoxicated problem drinker, he has demonstrated his unawareness of the real problems. If you yourself have alcohol troubles, or if someone in your family has, and you find yourself in the hands of a professional like this, get away quickly, so that at least you may save time and money. He has disqualified himself.

If, on the other hand, the professional gives evidence of attempting to detoxify the brain so he can deal with a body that is improving from a chemical and mechanical point of view, that person should not be ruled out, no matter how obnoxious he may appear on other grounds. (Remember that he may appear obnoxious only because he is disagreeing with your system.)

The helping person should recall at all times that his efforts must be directed at obtaining as large a time period free of alcohol as possible, and that it is in the client's best interest to increase the frequency and duration of these periods. Since most helpers are in the area because they really want to help, they must learn to resist the very natural tendency to try to be of assistance to the drinking person whenever he is in crisis. Since these crises so often revolve around the active use of alcohol, it is tempting to try to make sense to the drinking individual in order to help him. Generally, this is a waste of time; how can you make sense with a nonsensical person?

Since one reason for writing this book is to encourage beginners in the helping area and to show ways in which the success rates can become greater, it should not be considered a put-down that adherence to Myth II is one of the major mistakes made by beginners working in the field of alcohol problems. However, in most cases, a telephone call from an intoxicated client can be and should be handled by obtaining from the client as great a period of sobriety as is reasonably possible before the next interview. Thus, during "emergency" telephone calls from intoxicated clients, it will usually work very well for the helping person to take only one tack: "Have nothing further to drink until tomorrow morning"—if that is all you can squeeze out of the person at that time, or "Have nothing to drink for twenty-four hours and then call me," or other instructions in that general vein.

The drinker will generally exert a counterforce. As his befuddled brain registers it, he needs help at the moment, and generally he is in considerable very real distress. He is either crying or panicked and feels himself to be at the end of his rope. He has called in the first place because he thinks the helper will listen and support him in his time of trouble. There is a danger that the helping person can, by responding to this real need, actually encourage him to drink, since he will eventually learn that he gets more attention when he is in trouble than when he is doing well. You do not train a dog to stop biting by giving him a dog yummy every time he bites someone.

On the other hand, some of the oldtimers in the helping field, usually nonprofessionals, very helpfully give an active or obnoxious or really sick intoxicated individual *more* alcohol if that is the *only* way they can get him to a medical or other treatment facility. Such alcohol troubled persons often desperately require protection and treatment but don't pass out quite enough to get them "under cover."

The point here is that Myth II is counterproductive in most instances. Do not play psychotherapist with an actively drinking individual.

The number of emergencies that evaporate quickly once the active drinking ceases is amazing. Certainly, instructions

intended to support the individual in his attempts to stop
drinking (in order to talk to the therapist) should be
utilized. Usually, instructions to drink a lot of fluids and to
begin to force food seem to be helpful to individuals who are
trying to sober up enough to deal with the helper. Confused
or fearful people seem to respond well to brief, repeated,
simple instructions to perform some action to help themselves. Thus, instructions to perform some such action
should generally be interspersed with instructions to go out
immediately and buy, for example, two quarts of orange
juice that the drinker is to consume within the next twenty-
four hours. An interesting technique that seems to work
reasonably well for me is the following: Instruct the individual or the spouse to go and buy a couple of cans of sauerkraut, boil the contents in an equal amount of water, and
then strain off the resulting fluid. The sauerkraut juice is
to be put in the refrigerator and used to provide fluid and
also as a substitute should the urge to drink strike again.

For some reason, this works reasonably often, particularly with problem drinkers who are enamoured of beer;
whether it works on some chemically corrective basis, or
because the tart taste substitutes somehow for the beer
taste, or whether its effectiveness is simply a function of
the helping person's giving some structure and urging self-
helping action, I don't know. The important thing is that
sometimes it helps. I frequently recommend instant chicken
noodle soup during these episodes simply because it provides
some nourishment and fluid in a form that seems to be tolerated by the drinker's queasy digestive system.

Since I have seen a number of patients with avitaminosis, which can express itself in a variety of ways, one of
which is a brain condition caused by lack of necessary vitamins, and since many alcohol-damaged people for some
reason shy away from eating vegetables, I also like to recommend that the individual coming off alcohol buy a head of
lettuce and take a bite of that at least once a day. This is
not a substitute for therapeutic vitamins, of course. Again,

these techniques seem to work with some patients, possibly because it gives them something to do to help themselves rather than to feel completely at the mercy of their condition. Maybe it feels like a form of magic—OK, I'll use that too.

It should be remembered that dangers are present at this juncture and for seventy-two to ninety-six hours thereafter. Some of these dangers will be discussed in the section on DTs in Chapter 4.

There is one other major exception to the general rule of not wasting time (or of using your time negatively) with the troubled person who is currently drinking. Sometimes one can gain an initial grip on the unconvinced alcohol troubled person when he is really suffering in the acute throes of discomfort and guilt from the alcohol ingestion. Sometimes when he is in trouble and is intoxicated he can be told that he is in trouble and will recall some of it later. Usually, however, the most useful time to attempt to engage the unconvinced person in a treatment effort is within the first three days after cessation of the drinking behavior. The first day is probably better than the third, but in any event what the helper is trying to do is to drive a wedge into the system by beginning to talk with the individual when he is feeling guilty, or tearful, or frightened, and when he is hurting and tremulous.

We all have short memories. The alcohol-damaged person seems to be afflicted with a shorter memory than most of us; after the three days, if he has not gone into DTs, he tends to heal over and to be less distressed by his self-destructive, pain-producing behavior. He has, in effect, once again forgotten how lousy he felt three days ago. If one can intervene during the discomfort period, however, one can sometimes be quite helpful.

To the person who has been turned off by whoever has been attempting to help, I would simply suggest that your anger is usual and to be expected. If you are irritated by the helper's apparently callous abandonment of you in your time of need, your reaction is quite usual and the helper knows very well that you will dislike him for it. He is willing to accept this from you. On the other hand, the helper is trying to do what is most useful to you in both the short run and the long run, even though he has not immediately pleased you by his refusal to deal with you when you are drinking. It is also obvious that if you really don't like this kind of behavior from your therapist or other helper, you always have the option of dealing with him sober.

Myths I and II have an interesting corollary. Increasingly, I find it amazing that professionals, especially mental health professionals, who are dealing with depressed patients do not automatically attempt to estimate the extent to which that individual is drinking. I once worked on a psychiatric ward on which a depressed patient regularly conducted drinking parties late at night, unknown to the major portion of the treating staff, who failed to note that alcohol problems were causing the depression.

Since depression is a major psychological and psychiatric problem, it is also likely to be present in many physical disorders encountered by the general practitioner. Such "masked depressions" may be expressed as generalized pain, headaches, inability to breathe properly, and other symptoms.

The pure and inescapable fact is that a person who has any significant depression should decrease the amount of his drinking, whether or not he otherwise has a problem with alcohol. The chemical alcohol simply makes people feel more depressed, and this effect can persist for several days after the last drink.

If a therapist or helper is alerted to the fact that increased depression follows significant drinking, he can begin to check out alcohol intake in depressed persons and can do a number of useful things. At the very least, the individual's alcohol intake should be cut at least in half and preferably eliminated completely as an experiment in well-being conducted mutually by the treater and the treated.

For people who have a couple of cocktails at night but who have difficulty sleeping in the early morning hours, who have trouble making decisions during the day, or who show other signs of depression, an experiment of about three weeks of alcohol abstinence is a small price to pay for increased ease. Generally patients undergoing such an experiment will get visible and significant, if perhaps only partial, relief from their depressive symptoms and will begin to notice the advantages of decreasing the intake. Again, this discussion of depression does not apply only to problem drinkers, but to anyone who is carrying an uncomfortable load of depression. Thus, while it does not make sense to talk at great therapeutic length to people who are actively drinking, it makes equally little sense to attempt to treat depressives without attending to their alcohol intake.

In my practice as a clinical psychologist, I must confess that I am often secretly a little pleased to find a measurable intake of alcohol in someone who is depressed, since it gives me a very rapid means of improving the situation for the patient.

There is a Mark Twain story that goes something like this: Mark Twain fell ill and went to his physician, who urged him to give up smoking, drinking, and chasing after women. He did so (I assume for only as long as his health required) and recovered. Not long after, a spinster friend of his fell ill. Since she indulged in no vices she could not give them up and was like a sinking ship with nothing to jettison to lighten her load. She died.

I do not urge persons who are depressed to take up the banner of strong drink in order to feel better by giving it up. But many people who are in depressive episodes have discovered that the pain of the depression is momentarily eased by a little alcohol. What they don't know is that drinking will make them feel worse a few days later when it is difficult to connect the drink and the feeling.

I feel a little down myself after all that depressing talk, and the Mark Twain story forces me to tell this:

A man went to his physician and asked for the formula to reach one hundred years of age. He, too, was told to give up smoking, drinking, and chasing after women. "Will I live to be a hundred?" he asked.

"No," said his doctor, "but it will seem like it."

It seems a shame that "chasing after women" tends to get lumped in this kind of story with enterprises as unhealthy as smoking and drinking.

Myth III:
The Need for "Motivation"

The third myth holds that the problem drinker cannot help himself or be helped unless he has somehow determined for himself voluntarily that he wants to.

The first two myths are almost exclusively the province of professional helping people who have read a lot of theory written by people like themselves—uncritical, inexperienced theory-makers and theory-believers. Myth III spreads out to nonprofessional helpers, most notably the old hands in Alcoholics Anonymous (AA) or the new ones who have heard the old line.

Myth III comes in two basic forms, which are actually identical, despite the different phraseology:

Myth III, Form A.   In "old-line" AA form, this myth holds that the individual suffering from alcohol abuse has to "hit bottom." Essentially this signifies that he has to have "hit his own bottom"—or come to suffer badly enough to "really" want help, whatever "really" may mean.

In professional mental health circles, Myth III (Form *B*) is couched in "motivational" terminology. Phrases like "truly motivated," "willing to work in therapy," and "internal motivation" are popular. This nonsense is found not only with regard to alcohol, but also when "motivation for therapy" for almost any emotional difficulty is considered. It gets the pressure off everyone but the sufferer.

The only reasonable answers to Myth III are to suggest to the one group that they think about finding ways to define bottom earlier and higher; and to the other group that they start thinking about whether the concept of motivation in this sense is in fact useful.

In the mid-1960s, a number of people interested in alcohol problems began, independently, to develop the notion that perhaps alcohol problems could be tackled earlier. If so, the individual troubled by the problem might not have to lose and/or blight his family, his job, his health, or his self-respect. Why, the reasoning went, should the process be attacked only after most of the strengths in a person's life are gone?

This thinking was most unpopular in AA circles at that time, and still is in some places—perhaps more accurately, in most places by some AA people. On the other hand, in the early '70s, one began to hear (or at least I did) among younger AA members, usually out of earshot of the "hardliners," that "bottom" could be set higher. Things could be done to intervene earlier. People who seemed to be in early trouble could be given information. They could be assisted more actively to go to AA earlier, and, when there, could be excused from matching "horror" stories with other AA members. Those colorful tales of life difficulties—often including jail, repeated hospitalization, crime, pain inflicted on loved ones—were not designed to be matched, or to be told with pride, but to be helpful. Many individuals going to AA for the first time with the beginnings of a problem were leaving, saying (incorrectly), "I can't have an alcohol problem; I've never had problems like that." They were, in short, driven away by their inability to top the other guys' drinking.

As they failed to return, in droves, the "ins" shook their heads sagely and confided to one another that the non-returners weren't "ready yet" or hadn't "hit bottom." "They'll be back when they're hurting enough."

A lot of them died, and are dying yet, before they can get back.

I do not wish to be misunderstood. I believe that AA is a magnificent fellowship and a fine organization—for some people. I have been moved to tears by the beauty of some of its doings, some of its members, and some of its results. Always, there have been AA people who have reached out to help before a person knew he needed it, or before he knew what to do about his need. That is hard work, and personal risks of facing anger and rebuffs—and of not always being liked—have to be taken.

But the notion of the "low bottom" and letting people slide to it unaware and uninformed and unsupported is destructive and unnecessary.

If you are reading this because you suspect a problem in yourself or in a family member, do not turn away from AA because of my concerns—they are voiced in the hope that AA will become even better. The young people, and the new people, and some of the old hands who are flexible enough to try new ways, and yourself, if you will enter in and get sober, can help set a new, more hopeful "bottom."

If alcohol trouble is a sickness—what treatable sickness or disease is best arrested by letting it go until the patient is dead or almost destroyed? If it is a compulsion—what compulsion is best treated by letting it harden and crystallize for ten years when the problem is clear in two? If it is an addiction—what addiction is broken better later than earlier?

Who has a better chance at recovery, the skid row bum who has little body, little brain, little youth, little self-respect, no family, a desolate work history, few resources in general—or the guy who has all these things left to him but is on a track to lose them? And I will not concede that the bum has no chance, but I know his chance is statistically slimmer and his road back longer and rockier.

To the AA member who believes in the "low bottom" theory: Please look again, even if *you* yourself had to go through the fire. This is not a fraternity initiation.

To the AA member who tries in his actions to help

others avoid the low bottom, but who inconsistently talks the low bottom: Cut it out; it is damaging to those around you. Some people, out of anger and rejection, will abandon the early problem drinker, partly because, with your unthinking talk, you give them an excuse to misunderstand.

Closely akin to the thinking that permits the lonely and painful slide to the bottom is the thinking that "real alcoholics" cannot be helped by simple, straight information. Since "alcoholism" is a sneaky beast and builds up in subtle, cumulative ways, often in social drinking situations, many among us develop serious drinking problems unwittingly. Many people who meet all the criteria of "alcoholics" simply stop when informed by a knowledgeable person. This may occur in a physician's office at an annual checkup; through a clergyman's intervention at the request of a spouse; in a mental health clinic; in a hospital bed following an alcohol-associated admission for, say, pneumonia, malnutrition, or DTs; through an AA member's alertness. A person can end up in quite advanced stages of alcohol troubles in this society without being aware of it.

It is useful for us to learn that many genuinely serious alcohol problems are soluble. To hear that an individual in serious difficulty simply stopped drinking, it seems to me, could more profitably call forth a response of "Great" than a sour "He didn't really have a problem, then."

I smoke too many cigarettes, a habit I dislike in myself. I am, I fear, a nicotinoholic. Occasionally I run into someone who, for example, got up one night in a coughing fit, went out for a walk, lit up a cigarette, started coughing, threw the pack off the bridge, and says, "And I haven't had a cigarette since that moment."

I'm pleased for him. A little envious too. I used to look for outs for me, until I found that sometimes these better-than-me's had smoked more cigarettes for more years than I. Less addicted? Nope.

Now I've grown enough to be pleased that it can be done, and that here in front of me is someone apparently no brighter, or stronger, or more worthwhile than I, who has made it. Rather than wriggle and squirm trying to prove to myself that his problem was, after all, nowhere near as epic and heroic a one as my own, I can now accord him or her the respect I truly feel underneath my false pride. Their example gives me hope that I can do it some day, for they are not all *that* much better than I.

Myth III, Form B.   A significant portion of my life is devoted to training graduate students in clinical psychology. These are highly selected, extremely bright people. They have survived the scholar's trials—they were not weeded out of our education process when they turned sixteen, nor did they have to go to work after high school. They were admitted, after much competition, to colleges, usually pretty good ones, which they survived in good order. Then they applied to graduate schools and were selected for our Ph.D. program—about one out of one hundred applicants is accepted.

After all this selection I am stunned each year when a new batch of them comes into my course in psychotherapy —their heads are simply not screwed on straight with regard to "motivation," as it has come to be called in my racket. They cannot and do not think critically, or with flexibility or common sense about "motivation." They share these traits with many therapists who are out in the field, having completed their training and gained extensive experience.

Sadly, it appears that we might best throw away the term "motivation." It has been a comfortable security blanket, perhaps, for helper-type people, but a close examination of what we do with the concept reveals that in practical situations it is useless. Sometimes it is worse than useless; rather, it is more of a hindrance because it obscures and seems to explain more than it actually does. This problem, we will see, is precisely the same as the "low bottom" issue, and the idea of "being ready."

All of us, "alcoholics" and "nonalcoholics" alike, mental

health professionals and laymen, seem to need the patient's or other person's "genuine" or "real" or "personal" commitment. "He doesn't really want to stop drinking yet" is, after all, no different from "His motivation is poor."

The hard facts of the matter are that no person with a drinking problem, and no individual with a neurotic outlook on life "really" (that is, totally and without reserve) wants to change. Mostly what he wants is to be able to continue as he is but to pay either a smaller price or no price, against all the evidence of his senses.

This is simply another way of saying that the senses of alcohol troubled persons aren't very good after all, or at least that they are not the same as our (helper's) senses and viewpoints. Thus we hear, "If only I could learn to eat when I'm drinking I would be all right." Or the story, probably apocryphal, about the man who drank a quart of scotch a day, found himself not surprisingly in some difficulty, and convinced himself that hard liquor is worse for you than beer. He translated the alcohol content of a quart of scotch into beer, and found that in 2½ gallons of beer a day there was an alcohol content equivalent to that in his daily scotch quota. Three days later he found himself again in the gutter, and then, still not having learned, began translating into wine. Or the woman whose physician prescribed a tranquilizer to help her through alcohol withdrawal, telling her the two didn't mix, so she gave up the tranquilizer.

The point is that people in trouble with booze are in conflict—ambivalent—torn between drinking and not drinking. Thus, when they earnestly tell you they "really" are going to stop now, because they "really" want to, in themselves and for nobody else and with no bad motives, they are telling the truth—as far as it goes. The rest of the truth, hidden from them at the moment, is that they also want very much to continue to drink. It is hard to lose an old friend and protector, even after it begins to change and do you in. It is difficult to imagine a rewarding life without it and all the joys it has brought. It is, in the jargon of my profession, "overlearned behavior." In lay language it's a big habit.

If somebody shows up at a mental health clinic or a psychiatrist's office for an emotional problem, or at AA, he has already generally made a big (although ambivalent) decision. It is a big step.

Now Joe Big-Step enters the helper's office. The helper wants to know somewhere in the interview, either directly or indirectly, whether the "motivation" is proper. Is the motivation strong enough, is it "honest," or is Joe Big-Step in there for some less-than-good reason? Is he, in short, a clear-thinking, sturdy, well-integrated individual who will start in treatment "for himself," or is he, on the contrary, arriving at the helper's place of business to keep his wife happy, or convince a judge or employer of his good intentions? Is he, in essence, really a volunteer?

It is safest and most intellectually honest to realize that the person seeking help probably is not a volunteer in the usual sense of the word. It is safe to assume that he has arrived because something has screwed up his drinking pattern and turned it into something more painful than he had bargained for. Perhaps a judge *has* sent him to your mental hygiene clinic, or the local chief of police *has* threatened to charge him unless he goes to AA, or his wife *has* threatened again (but this time she sounded as though she meant it) to kick him out of the bosom of his family, or his belly hurts, or he ran out of money and strength, and so on.

At one time I developed and directed an alcoholism unit in a general medical hospital to which were referred individuals identified by the treating physician as people in serious trouble (physical, at the very least) with alcohol. Almost none of them was a volunteer in the usual sense, but we talked to them, informed them, urged them to sit in on our treatment efforts. Sometimes we were party to coercion in which the physician said, "Either go to that unit, which you need, or we will discharge you tomorrow."

We have uncovered no hard data whatever suggesting that the volunteer does better than the nonvolunteer. I defy anyone else to come up with such data, and I submit that it is a serious misuse of our already limited personnel resources to attempt to winnow out the nonvolunteer. Even those who temporarily make the right verbal noises—"I really mean it this time; I'll do anything"—are not volunteers. They are almost without exception forced into treatment by some life circumstance.

In "other-drug" circles there are two approaches to motivation. It has been a fad in these circles to "weed out" those who are not seriously motivated by interposing artificial and arbitrary barriers between the person to be helped and the drug treatment house he wants to get into. To determine that he has the right motivation, he may be required to call on the telephone every day at a certain, usually inconvenient, time, and beg for admission. (Community mental hygiene clinics also play this game in a modified form—usually the prospective client is required to set up his own appointment in order to "ensure" at least a bare minimum of good motivation. This holds even if he has a telephone phobia or is so depressed he can't use the phone.) The prospective drug client then has to meet other dehumanizing conditions—"If he will take this then we can have our way with him and therefore help him."

Another school of thought holds that one should "motivate" drug-dependent people by means of strong legal threat. Under the Big Club method, an individual is sentenced to a prison term varying between about four and forty years. The sentence is then remitted as long as the "helpee" remains in good standing in, for example, the local residential drug program. Such a Big Club motivational system operates in my own state; the motivators are repeatedly stunned by the large proportion of persons who try the drug program and within days, weeks, or months consciously opt to leave and start serving their ten-year stretch. What could clearly motivate the judge and other nonprisoners regularly fails to motivate the people they're dealing with.

Since we are all people of good intent, we accept that these two disparate systems—the Fight-to-Get-In and the Big Club techniques—are exercised by people who mean well. Both fail far more than they succeed; neither technique recommends itself significantly more than the other. It is probably true that each method drives away different kinds of people, and does, indeed, help others, but too few others.

Since approximately 40 to 50 percent of people who initially contact mental health clinics do not continue beyond one to three sessions, it appears that we are all doing something wrong with regard to our old beliefs about motivation.

I suggest that we are far wiser to stop screening out on the basis of inadequate motivation, and to find, instead, positive ways of conceptualizing the isues so that we may capitalize on the assets of people who have taken the frightening Big Step of dealing with us for the first time. If our limited time were redirected toward simply helping people return for as long as they need to, we would use it far more profitably.

A pretty good rule of thumb is: If he will suffer your presence, he is "motivated." Or if he is with you physically, you can do your job.

Whether you are a helper or a person who wants help, or the spouse of an alcohol-damaged person—don't spend so much time and energy worrying about whether he or she or you are "really serious" or will be at some time in the future if certain unspecified things occur or don't occur. If you're there, or he or she is there, the motivation is sufficient.

The motivation is probably mixed at best, and is accompanied by a wish not to be there or to thwart the progress of the treatment. Despite the negative feelings, you have enough to work with; the fact that the positive feelings outweigh the negative is attested by the mere presence of the person to be helped.

I am reminded of vocational aptitude testing to determine whether someone can learn to be a good typist. Sometimes it makes sense to spend equivalent time teaching the person to type rather than performing tests. If you want to know whether someone will return for further sessions, make it as possible as you can for him or her to return and then, mutually and definitely, make another appointment. If they don't show, (1) you have somehow messed it up and (2) you can do some of that paperwork you hate so much.

Myth IV:
"All Alcoholics Are Liars"

Myth IV states that the alcohol troubled person denies he has an alcohol problem in order to protect his habit, because "alcoholics are liars," because he is not yet motivated to attack the problem, because he is negativistic and obnoxious, and so forth. It is my position that, until the alcohol troubled person is *informed* about the alcohol issues and the ways in which he or she is *specifically* affected by them, we can no more call him or her a denier than we can call the average mental health professional a denier; neither recognizes the problems, simply because our folkways and attitudes and myths as a general society becloud our vision.

Most people think of "an alcoholic" as someone who drinks almost everyday, looks and acts erratic and sick, is a bum and never works, and is often intoxicated. As subsequent chapters will show, huge numbers of people who are in extreme difficulty with alcohol meet *none* of these criteria. Typically, if an individual in such great trouble were to go to a mental health clinic for, let us say, alcohol-induced depression, the mental health professional would miss the problem unless the person arrived obviously intoxicated or unless he announced, "I am an alcoholic." *Even then*, unless the person were slovenly, poor, or in an otherwise ob-

viously one-down position, it is reasonably likely that the
mental health worker would deny the contribution of alcohol to the problem. The reason is that typically the connections are *not known* to us. Why should the mental health
professional (almost always untrained in alcohol matters)
know things that the society does not know? And if the
helper doesn't know (because the client fails to fit a false
stereotype), how can we reasonably expect the client to
know?

Further, if in an effort to get a better picture of John
Smith's drinking pattern, we ask Mrs. Smith whether he
drinks, she is very likely to say, "Well, he drinks some, but
he's not an alcoholic!" She may say this for a number of
reasons: (1) She would be ashamed if he were; (2) she, like
John himself, is not informed about alcohol danger signs;
(3) John drinks at the same rate and the same times, and
consumes the same beverage, that she and all their friends
do. He may only rarely become intoxicated, not drink every
day, and so on. What we know that she doesn't know is that
even within these circumstances he may be in desperate
trouble. Perhaps he metabolizes at a different rate than
she, or has been at it over a longer span of time, or eats
differently, or for another reason is being affected adversely.

We—the alcohol sufferer, the spouse, the mental health
helper—are easily misled by our poor store of information
and inaccurate perceptions of what constitutes an alcohol
problem.

Not long ago I was asked to speak on alcohol problems
to the staff of a large community mental health center. All
seemed attentive enough, and some were even enthusiastic.
As usual, I included a discussion centering on the high
percentage of the average mental health clinic adult population that can be expected to have alcohol involvement
(about 50 percent), and the forces that militate against
accurate identification of these problems. Members of the
staff and I even went through part of the caseload, applying the tests I had shown. All agreed that this was a new

and helpful way to approach the problem and that they had not previously had the data, skills, and outlook to spot people troubled by alcohol. Near the end of the conference a bright, middle-aged psychiatrist asked in exasperation, "Why don't they *do* something about their drinking, then, rather than come in here? When we ask them if they're alcoholics, they almost always say no."

I gave him the only possible answer. "They're not trying to fool you," I said. "They don't know any more than you did before today's discussion. If *you* don't know how to spot alcohol troubles, as you agreed was the case before we talked today, how can you expect clients to tell you? They haven't had your medical school and other training, and even if they had, we cannot expect that it would have informed them any better than it informed you."

The plain fact is that plain facts are not widely available, and that laying them out permits substantial numbers of alcohol troubled people and others to perceive issues more clearly. There are, to be sure, blockages sometimes. Generally we can assign responsibility for the slowness of understanding to long overlearned, inaccurate habit; if one hears something enough times and if the general consensus seems to support the misconception, it is only human nature to accept it as a truth.

If the so-called alcoholic seems to deny that he has a problem, it is clearly legitimate to inform him, give him some facts and suggest some profitable ways of viewing the issues. If he continues to reject your pieces of information, you can begin to consider denial as a mechanism. That some alcohol troubled people deny in the classical sense of the term is irrefutable, particularly when severely troubled and chronically embroiled. Much more often than we expect initially, however, they are, like the rest of us, simply badly informed.

I offer a vignette, one of many possible, to support my position. In a class dealing with the alcohol troubled person, a young man interrupted about halfway through the semester. He was hesitant at first, but when he realized that it

was OK for him to talk, he became more confident and
fluent. He said that he was twenty-eight and had served as
a Marine in Vietnam without sustaining injury to himself
except to get turned on to alcohol and other drugs. After
his discharge he obtained employment as a mechanic, but
he had always wanted to work with people and had enrolled
in the present course to begin preparation for a people-help-
ing job. Suddenly, he said, during a lecture the previous
week, a stunning awareness had "washed over" him. He,
himself, of all people, was in significant trouble with alcohol!

The male members of his family had always been hard
workers and hard drinkers in the sporadic, binge fashion.
A favorite uncle had died of cirrhosis. The young man had
begun to frequent a local watering hole that was favored by
the college crowd—a spot famous for heavy drinking and
frequent fights. Upon leaving one night he ran his car at
high speed into a stone wall on a curve. Taken to the local
hospital, he received emergency care and, due to the severity
of his condition, was transferred to a city hospital having
more comprehensive resources. From there he was sent to
the regional Veterans Administration Neurological Unit.

He was comatose for about two weeks, and when he
regained consciousness he gradually realized that he had
sustained a broken shoulder and cheekbone and the permanent loss of sight in one eye. His memory for the accident and events prior to it was gone, and he had recon-
structed those events from the accounts of others. He was
unable to read, write, or speak, and tried suicide by attempting to leap from a window. Restrained from that, he
was transferred to the closed psychiatric unit where he received treatment for six weeks. "Last week in class," he
concluded, "I realized that I was still drinking in the way
I was drinking when I had the accident—I never connected
those troubles with drinking."

Was this denial? I don't think so. If it was denial in a
classical sense, why relinquish it merely because of the infusion of some relevant information? And why, pray tell,

did none of the staff of the psychiatric unit utilize some of those six weeks to impart the information and help form the connection?

I urge those of my readers who are in helping professions to try the information route before settling on the denial ploy. I believe your experiences will be like mine and you will perceive much less denial than you do now.

So much for Myth IV.

3
Helpful and Unhelpful Definitions

an old stomach
reforms more whiskey drinkers
than a new resolve
and the sexton
stops more than either
> From *the life and times*
> *of archy and mehitabel*
> Don Marquis

No reasonable doubt remains that we have expended, and continue to expend, tremendous amounts of energy on discussing and worrying about the *severely* alcohol troubled person in our society, almost to the exclusion of the much more common, and only partially damaged, individual and family. It is with trepidation that I share some of my concerns in regard to the words we utilize when talking about alcohol troubles; to swim against a strong current is hard work.

To be more than superficially involved in alcohol work is to find oneself immersed in a sea of denial and misunderstanding generated, and constantly revealed, by others.

Certainly, having been raised in precisely the society that breeds this strange difficulty, even he who is strongly interested and informed is subject to the denial and distortion he sees in others. I consider myself to be no exception—the most I can say is that I am working on it.

I have repeatedly been in gatherings at which alcohol-wise members of the group—totally separated psychologically from the rest—have exchanged glances with one another meaning "Here we go again. They've denied and twisted the way they usually do." This happens, as a general rule, in such stock situations as meetings with mental health professionals, when too often the self-proclaimed experts begin pontificating about how one gets rid of the "underlying pathology before attacking the alcoholism" (see Myth I). Then we know they haven't heard what we know and that, worse, their needs to talk about a system that *never has worked* far outweigh their abilities to learn new material and a new set of feelings.

But if the truth were told, the same kind of sly splintering also occurs between groups of so-called alcohol experts. Certainly some AA people feel themselves to be set apart from some non-AA people. Certainly some non-AA people who are knowledgeable about alcohol feel the same way about some AA people. And I, sometimes in the company of people who believe as I do, have felt myself to be a part of a secret "We know and they don't" conspiracy.

The Problem of Definition

I suggest that we are in a struggle of words, of semantics, that are at the service of an underlying attitudinal problem; the words express the struggle, and often, it seems, partially cause it. If our major task is to alter the attitudes so that we can all be more productive—and I believe that is our major task—then we must attend to the semantics. We must somehow do so, however, without losing sight of the fact that it is not the semantics that we should worry about, but rather the attitudes underlying the choice of words.

A useful concept here is that of "excess meaning" in the use of language. In brief, one can select words, often without consciously intending to, that carry not only cognitive or informational meaning but also an emotional connotation. Thus, "You are stubborn, but I am persistent" manages a good deal of excess meaning and not only bespeaks a given attitude but also shapes and supports the very existence of the attitude.

The terms *alcoholism* and *alcoholic* have acquired a heavy excess meaning value in American usage, and I wish to explore the knotty and sensitive question of whether we must consider dropping the terms. Ideally in such an enterprise one should attempt to substitute a more useful term; the best I have come up with is "the alcohol troubled person," which is a trifle unwieldy but descriptive. One of my students came up with "the ATP," which eliminates the unwieldiness, forces one to learn the system, and retains accuracy.

I have long since, and with reluctance, come to a specific and definite difference of opinion with AA on the concept of whether it is always or even often helpful to force an alcohol troubled person or ATP to admit he is "alcoholic." There is no question in my mind that this can be helpful to some alcohol troubled persons—for them it is OK. But large numbers of people—in my terms often those in minimal or moderate trouble—are in fact turned off and driven away from the otherwise helpful AA system by the term "alcoholic," which in present usage is saturated with excess negative meaning.

Heaven only knows how difficult it can be to break through the denial in an *individual* ATP and to make it possible for him or her to become engaged in some form of useful intervention. But that's easy compared to helping a *group* of executives, or judges, or plant superintendents to

accept and understand alcohol issues. Or psychiatrists, or
psychologists. Or any *group* of Americans.

Today the term "alcoholic" seems to flip a switch that
makes people think "skid row" or "severely damaged" or
"bum" when you're trying to get them to deal with "minimal" or "prevention" or "help people in your court" or
"many people with alcohol troubles are helped right away
if you, the helper, will only address the issue straight and
fast in an informed, unembarrassed way."

If we try to hang the label "alcoholic" on someone who
will necessarily and predictably have to deny it because the
very word dredges up awful images, maybe we are attempting to be clever or one-up rather than helpful.

Once I was in charge of a ward in a psychiatric hospital
and one of the patients, a young man, was pretty confused.
We believed that patients on the unit would benefit by helping with the housekeeping. Bill's response was always a
hostile, "This is a hospital; I don't have to do your work
for you." One day I relabeled the whole mess and suggested
that he was right and I wasn't urging any work on him, but
would he be willing instead to mop his corridor every morning? "Sure," said he, and did it happily.

Work is one thing, a little mopping quite another.
Words are funny things.

A lot of money and programs is flowing right now
in the name of alcoholism, and far be it from me to jeopar-
dize such a welcome and (in alcohol work) new state of
affairs. This money labeled "alcoholism" money has flushed
out of the woodwork any number of instant experts and
programs, but if, in the long run, more people get informed,
alerted, and interested that way, it's really a good thing.

Even though I hate to rock the boat under these new
and funded circumstances, I believe we need some new directions to make the greatest possible progress.

You will note, then, that although I occasionally use
the words *alcoholic* and *alcoholism*, something like *alcohol
problems* or *ATP* is much more often used. This practice is

in keeping with the conviction that to use the old terms is to perpetuate our attitudinal difficulties because there is so much negative excess meaning attached to them that by using them we actually mislead one another.

Still, the word *alcoholic* has served us well until now, or maybe until ten years ago, because people concerned about other human beings in trouble with alcohol could rally 'round the word and keep helping efforts alive, and those long-term efforts have led to our present situation of guarded optimism.

There are many possible definitions of an "alcoholic." I have taken the stand that the very use of the term may well be causing more trouble than it's worth, because it often generates such a frantic intellectual and emotional scrabbling to make sure the word can't be applied to *us* or anybody *we* know or live with.

The main business of this chapter is to sample the many definitions that are current; the sampling is not all-inclusive but is representative. We will find that some definitions are not true, that some lend themselves peculiarly to a continuation of troubled drinking, and that others are poor for a combination of reasons.

Others have much to commend them in that they help some people and thus pass the ultimate pragmatic test of usefulness.

I insert here a definition that I believe to be superior to others; amplification and discussion of this definition in fact constitute the next chapter:

An individual has troubles with alcohol if he or she continues to drink when to do so reduces the quality of his or her life in any one (or more) of the following four areas:
1. *Social (including, but not confined to, family)*
2. *Financial (including, but not confined to, job)*
3. *Physical*
4. *Emotional and Cognitive.*

Please note immediately that (1) intoxication has nothing whatever to do with this definition and (2) all we are saying is that if you have troubles with alcohol you have troubles with alcohol. If so, you ought to look at your problems, and to help you do so fruitfully we provide a convenient four-part breakdown and a structure.

I submit that a good definition should have the following characteristics:

1. It should be simple, easy to remember, clear, and straightforward.
2. It should be consonant with reality.
3. It should break down factual inaccuracies and counterproductive attitudes toward alcohol problems.
4. It should in and of itself provide useful information.
5. It should enable the alcohol troubled individual and his family, and their potential helpers, to notice and identify the problem sooner and with greater clarity.
6. The definition should not unnecessarily raise defenses and should thus assist in achieving a desirable reduction of anxiety, distortion, and denial. It should provide a logical tool for clinical treatment and for broad education. If we can avoid the pitfalls of defensiveness and the confusion bred by inaccuracy, there will be less need for the nonuseful, defensive kind of argument so often mounted by the alcohol-involved person, his family, his physician, his social worker, his boss, and so on.

I say this now so that you can apply these tests to the definitions as they appear.

Exclusionary Definitions

Everyone is entitled to his own beliefs in regard to deciding who has alcohol troubles. I would be pleased, of course, if you could end up using mine as a general map and retain others, or parts of others, that seem useful or emotionally satisfying to you, provided they are not among those that prove on examination to be particularly counterproductive and to cause nothing but grief.

In this category I place the highly defensive "exclusionary definitions" classically offered by the active alcohol troubled person or his family. I call such definitions exclusionary simply because the definer has a definition of his own that excludes himself and that alludes without quite saying so to a standard of "alcoholism" that is essentially "late stage" or severe. The exclusionary definition can be easily identified by inserting before it the words "I can't be an alcoholic because . . ." If that phrase sounds as if it would fit at the beginning of the definition, it has passed the test. Thus if one hears, "I have never missed a day of work because of drinking," simply insert at the beginning our test phrase "I can't be an alcoholic because . . ." and see how it sounds. The speaker is telling you that only alcohol-riddled losers miss work because of drinking—*that* is what constitutes a *true* "alcoholic"—and he's surely not one of those because he values the work ethic.

Here are some common exclusionary definitions.

Definitions Based on When One Drinks

Definitions based on *when* one drinks are patently absurd; they need to be rejected as masking the real difficulties, because they avoid the issues of trouble associated with drinking.

"(I can't be an alcoholic because) I never drink before breakfast (noon, supper, work, the crops are in, the kids are in bed)" and so forth is an old story to the alcohol worker on the firing line.

Why expend time and energy arguing, because who actually cares? Rather, learn to follow with, "Yeah, OK. But does it cause any *problems* even after you so carefully wait until some special tick of the clock?"

An important variant on the theme of *when* one drinks is the assertion that if you don't drink every day you can't have a problem, which is an exclusionary definition based on the common but erroneous belief that no alcohol troubled person can go twenty-four hours without a drink. Obviously

some can and some can't, because lots do and some don't.
Some drink only on weekends or are sporadic binge drinkers
or drink only when in port but never at sea or only at home
and never while performing surgery.

Definitions Based on Where One Drinks

Once, while following through on physicians' referrals
in a general medical hospital, I saw two different men in the
same day, one in the morning, the other in the afternoon.
Both had been hospitalized for serious medical consequences
of drinking and had started, medically, on the road to at
least temporary physical recovery.

The one in the morning solemnly assured me that he
couldn't have a problem because he drank only at home.
"I never go out to bars like those alcoholics do." In the
afternoon I was told by the other man, "I never bother my
family with it. I just drink at night in the bar."

That one taught me a lesson. Their enlarged livers
didn't know or care where the drinks that damaged them
were actually swallowed.

Definitions Based on With Whom One Drinks

The primary definition based on *with whom* one drinks
stems from the popular misconception that "real alcoholics"
always drink alone and are sneaky, devious, and secretive.
Some are and some aren't. Some are both, like the woman
who openly matches her guests drink for drink and sneaks
a little extra while in the kitchen hospitably getting refills.

The major variant on this theme is that if you're drinking with "class" people it's OK. So if the lawyer or legis-
lator drinks "only" with his colleagues, there can be no
problem. He figures that if everyone drinks together at
about the same rate, they're just meeting the social standard; the man who stops at the local bar with his co-

workers when the plant lets out feels the same way. Thus, if you don't lower yourself by "stepping down" for your drinking companions you're like everybody else. This argument tends to avoid the facts that some people get hurt on much less intake than others, that there is a tendency not to notice when one of the group drops out with ulcers, and that some colleagues drink additionally in other settings while others go home and have dinner with their families. People's life circumstances, bodies, and support systems are actually very different.

Definitions Based on What One Drinks

Other definitions are based on *what* one drinks. There is actually a widely held belief that drinking beer is not the same as drinking alcohol, and this misunderstanding is held, sometimes doggedly, even by people who are almost dead with it.

You need to be careful not to be taken in by the reasoning that one form of alcohol is more harmful, or more of an indication of problems, than another. Only in the case of fluids not considered beverages is this in fact true. People who drink shaving lotion, sterno, lab alcohol (unless a medical student), or antifreeze are clearly in real trouble with alcohol—and not only because some of them are drinking a form of alcohol that is a deadly and immediate poison (antifreeze, for example, is *not* ethyl alcohol, which we drink as a beverage).

"He has not stooped so low as to drink wine" is actually an exclusionary definition that completely ignores for the moment the competing evaluations of wine as a drink for the sophisticated, or for judicious use in the romantic interlude, or as an aid to philosophizing or digestion.

The topic of what one drinks seems especially well suited to exclusionary definitions: "All I drink is beer." "I never drink hard liquor." "I drink only good scotch." "I never drink alcohol straight." All of these can readily and comfortably be preceded by our exclusionary test phrase, "I can't be an alcoholic because . . ."

I got a call not long ago from an unsuccessful client (unless prolonging his life so someone wiser than I may eventually help him might be called a partial success) from six years ago. He had managed to drink himself into trouble again, with hard cider this time.

It really makes no practical difference what form the alcohol comes in. Even the woman who gets violent only on distilled spirits has a different kind of problem, but a real one nevertheless, when she drinks something else. Some people get headaches on wine and not otherwise. If there is no other accompanying problem, then a switch to something other than wine should reveal soon enough whether alcohol troubles exist. I know a woman who at one time was on the edge of alcohol troubles who is *truly* allergic to something in rye whiskey—a tiny sip makes her ghastly ill, crazy, and nonthinking. But larger amounts of alcohol in other forms do not affect her in that way.

Obviously, the concentration of alcohol (the proof, which amounts to twice the percentage of alcohol) varies for different drinks and may affect the speed with which an effect is felt.

But at base alcohol is alcohol, and the alcohol-damaged brain or body or career or family is not helped, but only further abraded, by alcohol intake in *any form*.

It is well to think of the name of the drink as saying something only about the fluid vehicle in which the alcohol is carried. The taste and concentration vary, of course, but no matter what evaluation otherwise is placed on, say, beer or bourbon or sherry, they are for our purposes simply all vehicles for alcohol.

Beginning helpers, including spouses and professionals, sometimes permit a certain amount of verbal jockeying, conning, and chivying to be foisted upon them in this regard. They may allow themselves to be convinced that a major improvement has occurred when Mary finally switches from scotch to "only" sherry and then expects to be treated as if this is a major accomplishment. Don't you believe it. She is either manipulating or is sincerely but invalidly convinced. You simply cannot drink and at the same time not drink. (For an exception to this general notion, note the Principle of Positive Movement, discussed in Chapter 8.)

There are several other exclusionary definitions. Again, you can always spot them by injecting the test phrase, "I can't be an alcoholic because . . ."

Psychoanalytic Definitions

Another completely unhelpful definition, although not an exclusionary one, arises out of the old Freudian psychoanalytic bag. It suffers because it (1) includes everyone and (2) has no helpful explanatory or treatment features. A description of the alcohol troubled person as having "an orally dependent character disorder" is simply hopeless as an explanatory concept. First of all, who isn't "orally dependent"? We all eat, right? Second, even if oral dependency were the exclusive preserve of the "alcoholic," how could that knowledge help him? Further, within the concept is embedded the term "character disorder," which translates in Psychiatrese to "hard or impossible to change," and hordes of ATPs are not at all hard to change—quite the contrary.

Definitional Progress

Progress has been made in one important definitional sense—namely, the standards used for diagnosis by the mental health professions as reflected in the bible of diagnoses of the American Psychiatric Association (APA). This document, on the desk of every establishment mental health professional, is called the *DSM*, or *Diagnostic and Statistical Manual of Mental Disorders*.

In the 1952 edition, psychogenic, or nonphysical, "alcoholism" fell under the category of "Sociopathic Personality

Disturbance," or individuals "ill primarily in terms of society and of conformity with the prevailing cultural milieu, and not only in terms of personal discomfort and relations with other individuals." "Alcoholism" was classified as an addiction under the "Sociopathic" heading. Total direct reference to alcoholism consisted of three lines, or about five-eighths of an inch of type.

In the 1968 revision of the *DSM*, psychogenic "alcoholism" falls under the heading of "Personality Disorders and Certain Other Non-Psychotic Mental Disorders," which strikes me as a modest improvement over "Sociopathic." In this revision "alcoholism" includes some elements I like to see, such as "damage their physical health, or their personal or social functioning." I do not like to see "A prerequisite to normal functioning," since I believe that the use of this chemical to achieve "normal functioning" is a contradiction in terms and also helps perpetuate the false belief that one has alcohol problems only if one acts as if one *needs* it.

Now the APA sees four subheadings under "Alcoholism"—"Episodic Excessive Drinking," "Habitual Excessive Drinking," "Alcohol Addiction," and "Other and Unspecified Alcoholism." That certainly reflects increased awareness, sophistication, and concern, which is definitely progress, since so many of the mental health professionals' patients have alcohol as a primary cause of their disorder. (Research suggests that perhaps 60 percent of adult inpatient first admissions to "psychiatric" facilities are alcohol-related.)

But now they would have us count the number of times per year ("as frequently as four" or "more than twelve") one gets intoxicated to help classify the disorder by subheading. Also, the alcohol problem remains clearly a "Mental Disorder," a conclusion with which I basically disagree.

Now we are up to about twenty lines of type specifically devoted to "Alcoholism"—almost five inches!

Although my phraseology sounds sarcastic, I am also

genuinely encouraged to see the additional interest in alcohol problems expressed in this document. I hope to see the eventual inclusion of warnings regarding alcohol usage inserted into many of the other psychogenic categories. Depressive reactions and the schizophrenias, for example, are often misdiagnosed because the alcohol intake has caused people to act crazy, and that fact is not registering widely among the pros.

In the portion of the *DSM* concerned with physical disorders, one also finds improved interest and sophistication. In 1952, under "Disorders Caused by or Associated with Impairment of Brain Tissue Function" we find one category, "Acute Brain Syndrome, Alcohol Intoxication," with about 2¼ inches of type, and under "Chronic Brain Disorders (Chronic Brain Syndrome Associated With Intoxication)" another 2½ inches.

The later edition lists under "Psychoses Associated With Organic Brain Syndromes" nine subheadings in about 13½ inches of type (two full pages), and one line appears in another section, "Non-Psychotic Organic Brain Syndrome with Alcohol."

The fact that there is no one definition embodying one universal and enduring truth is perfectly understandable and acceptable—we all know by now that there is no such thing as "an alcoholic" who can be unmistakably identified and relegated to one neat little cubbyhole. I would personally fight, and often do, to retain the differences of perception and belief in the field—if we all thought exactly alike we could not exchange ideas and improve our system. The diversity perhaps reflects the various points of view we bring to the problem—the psychologist puts his commitment to the psyche into it, and the clergyman generally includes the "spiritual" (which I am not personally driven to do although I have seen it done with excellent effect). The physician likes to emphasize medicine, and so forth.

Asking different professionals to define an alcoholic is somewhat like asking different people to describe a pigeon.

The gourmet attests that it is a delicious morsel; the city
sanitation engineer considers it a menace; the racing fancier
perceives it to be a computerized high-speed traveler; the
aeronautical theorist likes the relationship of mass to weight
and the lift provided by muscle and shape. The AA member
thinks it is somebody to be helped, about which more later.

Two More Definitions

While there is absolutely no way we can deal with all
the many definitions, at least two more need to be considered. One of these was suggested by Dr. Arthur Cain,
who in 1964 published a then-controversial book, *The Cured
Alcoholic* (J. Day Co., New York), which raised a storm
among some alcohol people, especially AA members, who
rightly perceived it to be a partial criticism of their fellowship. Cain selected a controversial title and did not hesitate
to take on AA as an adversary; various AA members re-
sponded, either angrily or thoughtfully. Those who were
angry and upset, and there was a goodly number of them,
had their own definitions of alcohol problems in their own
minds, and their definitions were at variance with Cain's.

Enough of a polarity was set up that the two viewpoints
can reasonably be discussed here in relationship to each
other.

Two statements are in order prior to the actual discussion. First, Cain's material deserves careful reading and
rereading. He neither elected me his defender nor seems to
need one, but as I have noted elsewhere we need diversity
of opinion right now. He helps provide it, and much of what
he says about alcohol problems makes great sense—to disagree about some aspects so completely that one cannot
digest the rest is not reasonable. I disagree, too, with some
of his positions.

Second, AA is composed of individuals, and among
those individuals are differences in viewpoint, so you cannot
always be sure that you are talking about an official position

when examining "AA" positions and feelings and interpretations. You tend to recall experiences and interpersonal interactions with individual members. In summary, AA does not always speak with one voice, although sometimes it does. And, just as I cannot fully accept all that Cain tells me, so I cannot fully accept all that AA people do. Both have made excellent contributions and it is my responsibility to note those contributions while carefully refraining from swallowing the whole package if it doesn't taste good to me.

A Definition Based on "Control"

Definitionally, Cain believes that he must ask: "Has this person lost control of his drinking?" This translates easily into "An alcoholic is one who has lost control of his drinking." It then follows that a "cured alcoholic" is one who can drink normally, which means, in turn, one who can again control his drinking. Additionally, "Normal drinking is any drinking that does not significantly alter the behavior of the drinker."

I wish Cain had let well enough alone and quit there. I would still mount the same argument against the "control" notion that I will later, but at least I wouldn't have to face the credibility gap created by this selection!

Now, may I suggest a general "rule of thumb" to illustrate what might reasonably be considered normal drinking:

An *apéritif* before dinner, to enhance the appetite: perhaps a dry vermouth; a glass of vin rosé; a Dubonnet on the rocks;

A glass of white wine with the fish course;

A glass of red wine with the meat course;

A liqueur after dinner: a cointreau, a créme de menthe, or other cordial;

A snifter of brandy at bedtime;

On special occasions, one or two whiskies and soda between dinner and bedtime.

I can only react by saying that if that's "normal" drinking, and one definitely gets the impression that he intends it as a possible standard daily dose, then I come from a different part of the world than he does.

One more quote: ". . . I must agree with Alcoholics Anonymous that the *uncontrolled* drinker is the only drinker properly categorized as an 'alcoholic.' "

Before I try to explain how AA defines alcoholism, I want to say the following:

There is no question in my mind that once in a long while an "alcoholic" quite worthy of the name drinks again without losing control and without making significant troubles for himself. But they are rare indeed. I know well one such person who is "high" in local AA circles (there *is* a pecking order, unofficially). He has been drinking wine with his evening meal for several years now—wouldn't admit it to an AA person and talks against it in public. There is, however, no advantage to him in drinking his wine in a controlled fashion, since, despite warm-sounding words like *cordial* and *apéritif*, nothing about alcoholic beverages makes them worth the risk he's taking.

Psychologists tell us that once you have established a habit, or have overlearned something, it is extremely easy to reactivate those overlearned responses if a situation arises that is similar to the one in which you learned them. If you're lucky enough to have reached fifty, and unlucky enough not to have ridden a bicycle since you were twenty, get on one again if you don't believe me. You may be a bit jittery and creaky, but isn't it amazing how quickly all those complex, simultaneous adjustments come back almost unbidden (especially if the bike is heading downhill instead of up)?

A woodsman would point out that you can sometimes locate old logging roads in the woods by glancing out of the corner of your eye, not head on. In direct vision there are too many big trees in the 150-year-old road, and your brain cannot overcome their existence in order to imagine the road. From the edge of your vision, the lay of the land and a fleeting, almost imperceptible something let you recreate the old trail. Even though you can't actually see it but must somehow sense it, you will discover that, once found, such roads and paths can be very quickly reclaimed by just a little use.

So goes the alcohol habit, once learned.

To continue to value alcohol consumption so much as to expend effort and put oneself in jeopardy to regain it makes about as much sense as pulling the pin on a hand grenade and playing catch with it. It might explode when it's high enough not to hurt you, but why play catch with an activated hand grenade? Can't you find a ball?

From the scientific, let's-learn-all-we-can-about-this-disorder perspective, Cain's point is worth making—maybe we can get some useful results from it some day. More knowledge is always better than less.

Cain and AA are entitled to their notion about "uncontrolled" drinking being the (or a) tip-off regarding alcoholism. If we define "alcoholism" that way, though, we fail to identify a huge number of alcohol-damaged people even though they are in significant trouble and need help. My definition says simply that if alcohol causes troubles in any one of the four areas listed, then alcohol is creating a problem. If you waste time deciding whether or not you or the person you're worried about is "controlled," you begin to stray from the issue and confuse yourself. Pretty soon you say, "I guess he's not an alcoholic because he never really goes overboard," and it's an easy step from there to "He doesn't have alcohol problems." All the time his liver is collecting more fatty tissue and getting bigger and functioning more poorly—and he is denied the opportunity of knowing what's killing him.

In short, control doesn't matter. Troubles matter.

AA Definitions

The AA literature, which represents the nearest we can come to an official position since it is cleared by a central AA General Service Conference and published by AA, has a number of definitions sprinkled throughout. In *Alcoholics Anonymous Comes of Age* we read about *"the obsession of the mind* that compels us to drink *and the allergy of the body* that condemns us to go mad or die." In the pamphlet *44 Questions and Answers About the AA Program of Recovery From Alcoholism* (1952), we read under "What Is Alcoholism?" that "The explanation that seems to make sense to most AA members is that alcoholism is an illness, a *progressive* illness, which can never be cured but which, like some other illnesses, *can* be arrested. Going one step further, many AA's feel that the illness represents the combination of a physical sensitivity of alcohol, plus a mental obsession with drinking which, regardless of consequences, cannot be broken by will power alone."

There is continual reference in AA literature and individual belief to such phrases as "compulsion to drink," "there is no such thing as being a little bit alcoholic," "an unmanageable problem," and "only the drinker can decide if he is an alcoholic."

Because of the importance of the AA movement, more is said of it elsewhere. Hopefully the general definitional stance of the fellowship has been made clear enough here for the reader who is not yet familiar with AA to get a partial feel until he can inform himself better through actually meeting AA people and perhaps going to some meetings.

For the moment, I will say that I have very little if any patience for the mental health professional, be he a psychologist, psychiatrist, psychiatric social worker, or whatever, who has not informed himself about AA, been to some meetings and found out, *for himself*, something about it. The number who have not is astounding and tragic, especially because these people deal so frequently with alcohol-damaged people whom they are treating as "depressives" or emotionally disturbed when the problem is a bad case of alcohol troubles. To remain uninformed is to be professionally irresponsible.

The family member who wants to help and/or be helped has absolutely no business trying to get daddy to the local AA meeting without having gone first. Al-Anon exists for spouses and AlaTeen for children of alcoholics.

I *always* refer alcohol troubled clients to AA immediately or as soon as they can accept it. I work very hard to help them get there, the sooner the better, despite the clear fact that I disagree with parts of AA's understanding of the problems.

Many people do very well when they get to AA; many cannot accept it but do well without it. While AA is often effective on the personal level for individuals, it has certainly not resolved society's alcohol problem (which is getting worse statistically) any more than I have, and its hit rate is lower than it needs to be (a problem that applies to all of us who labor in this particular vineyard, if you will forgive me for putting it that way). AA is a first line of defense and must *always* be tried, even though it is not the only avenue to help.

All of the definitions discussed here are used by various people to define "alcoholism." I do not wish to claim that no one but me has a good definition, yet some of the "guidelines" discussed here are counterproductive and give us difficulties. Others seem reasonable, but all are less useful than the definition to be examined more fully in the next chapter.

4
A Good
Working Definition

Start out with the conviction that absolute truth is hard to reach in matters relating to our fellow creatures, healthy or diseased, that slips in observation are inevitable, even with the best trained faculties, that errors in judgment must occur in the practice of an art which consists largely in balancing possibilities—start, I say, with this attitude of mind, and mistakes will be acknowledged and regretted; but instead of a slow process of self-deception, with ever increasing inability to recognize truth, you will draw from your errors the very lessons which will enable you to avoid their repetition.

Sir William Osler, 1892

Let us examine more closely the definition of alcohol troubles that was briefly presented in the last chapter as having great potential benefits in terms of comprehension, accuracy, lowering of defensiveness, and overall progress:

An individual has troubles with alcohol if he or she continues to drink when to do so reduces the quality of his or her life in any one (or more) of the following four areas:
1. Social (including, but not confined to, family)

2. *Financial (including, but not confined to, job)*
3. *Physical*
4. *Emotional and Cognitive.*

Such a person, within this system, would be viewed as an alcohol troubled person, an ATP, rather than an "alcoholic."

Social Components

The social area of one's life obviously includes family relationships but is not confined to how one gets along with one's kids or spouse. The ATP may not have any family. So social relationships necessarily include dealings with one's boss, fellow workers, neighbors, and many others.

The incautious use of alcohol leads some people to irascible behavior—a short temper, easy irritability, perhaps a readiness to react as if one is being picked on or misunderstood. It leads to wives being hospitalized for broken ribs (much more commonly than you might believe) or to children leaving home too early, having married or otherwise fled an intolerable situation.

The next chapter will deal with varying degrees of damage done to people's lives—it is vitally important to leave as much room in our thinking for the less severely damaged person or family as for the one that is almost destroyed by alcohol involvement.

Consider a family in which the wife, Mary, grew up with a father who drank heavily. Suppose that on pay nights he struggled home at 1:00 A.M., beat up the mother, and terrorized the children. Not a terribly unusual situation. In any event, Mary grew up, married, and had children of her own.

Mary's husband, Ralph, begins to stop off at the local pub one or two nights a week for about an hour to have a couple of beers. Although our definition does not ask how many is "a couple" (it is not always just two, as implied by the ordinary meaning of the term) and although it is not concerned with how big each beer of the "couple" is (a seven-ounce bar glass, a twelve-ounce bottle, a quart, a six pack, a keg), for the sake of discussion, Ralph has two six-ounce glasses, which amount to only a third of a quart and cost him maybe forty or fifty cents or less.

But Ralph comes home to Mary, supersensitized by her father's behavior to the smell of alcohol on a man's breath and frightened to death that Ralph, too, will "go bad." They argue. She says he's out entirely too much, that he smells like a barroom, that his children have a right to see their father more often and that in any event he is getting to be a lush.

Ralph responds with some justification that he's not drinking that much, that he's entitled to a little time with the boys and doesn't even go bowling any more lately, that he needs to unwind once in a while after a hard day's work, and anyway, that Charlie invited him and they're really getting friendly and Charlie's the foreman and Ralph will get ahead quicker this way.

It becomes a bit of a power struggle, with Mary unable to give in because of a terrible fear of which she may not even be aware, and Ralph unwilling to be controlled so stringently and unreasonably this early in the marriage. The argument grows more heated as Mary says "You always," and the children wake up. Ralph and Mary go to bed without touching one another—"I won't have anything to do with him when he's an animal like that"—and for the next couple of days Ralph is hurt and resentful, as is Mary. In that atmosphere they have disagreements about disciplining the kids, about how to spend their money, and about when they're going to visit her mother.

Finally they make up and exchange I'm sorry, honey's. That night Charlie asks Ralph to stop in at the Crystal Tap on the way home.

Ralph and Mary really do have some alcohol troubles. The troubles are not big yet, and they may never be. It accomplishes nothing to call Ralph an alcoholic, any more than it makes sense to say it's all Mary's problem. But this problem needs work before Ralph says the hell with it, I'll show her what too much is, or before she goes home to mother, or before the kids start crying themselves to sleep when they hear the arguments. No one in this family is addicted to alcohol, intoxicated, or spending too much money, but there are in fact alcohol troubles. Granted, there are also other difficulties in their relationship.

Why doesn't Ralph realize that Mary is scared to death of alcohol and take steps to reassure her? The argument that this is completely her hang-up won't wash. Like anyone else, she has hang-ups in other areas that he deals with and thus maintains a good relationship with her in those areas.

The point here is that for a couple of beers Ralph is putting a lot of trouble into his life. It does no good to argue that he is an alcoholic or that he is not, or that if Mary didn't have such a screwed-up background Ralph could have his two beers with no one injured. The fact remains that alcohol causes trouble between them. You might just as logically point out that if Billy Booze on skid row had a body that could handle alcohol better he could be as effective as his twin brother the excellent brain surgeon, who in fact drinks just as much as Billy.

Those arguments are sillily circular, as someone once expressed it to me. I can heartily agree that if things were different they'd be different. But since they aren't, we start at the beginning.

Ralph and Mary, plain and simple, are in trouble because of Ralph's two beers, among other things.

Ralph is not like some other guy who unfairly complains about his wife's cooking, housekeeping, personality, and figure until she fights back and gives him an excuse to stomp out of the house angry and go feed his habit at the local pub. But, of course, both constitute family troubles, which are included in the social area.

Family relationships are sometimes affected by alcohol

consumption subtly and sometimes strikingly. I recall two alcohol-damaged wives, each of whom had the misfortune to have a husband who unconsciously encouraged her drinking. The first was a grandmother with a history of repeated DTs and a badly damaged cirrhotic liver complete with swollen belly. Her husband liked to drink on Friday and Saturday evenings and continually arranged for her to come with him. He then bought her drinks, even when she had managed to achieve five days of sobriety. His behavior obviously cannot be used as an "out" for her—after all, one gives up self-destructive drinking for oneself—but it sure didn't help.

The second woman and her husband sat with me during an initial interview in which we talked about her problem and the attempt we would make together to dry her out without having to hospitalize her. This couple had it made financially, and among their other enterprises owned a fine restaurant to which they typically went to dinner on Sunday evenings. After our rather clear discussion the husband, probably believing he was being helpful, turned to his wife and said, "So this Sunday, honey, I'll have my cocktails and we'll just get a bottle of wine for you."

Each of these couples clearly had relationship problems. In each, the wife was in serious trouble and the husband was periodically enraged by her disturbed behavior after drinking. Neither husband was stupid, and I had to conclude that each had a hidden, unconscious need to do his wife in, so that each wife had to learn to handle her own problem in the direction of her own best interests.

On the other side of the coin we find the too-long-suffering spouse—sometimes a wife, sometimes a husband. The average spouse reaches a certain point at which separation or divorce in the face of a continuing alcohol problem makes excellent sense, especially if the alcohol troubled partner makes no sturdy attempt to change. Such decisions are infinitely more difficult and complex, however, when the alcohol-involved partner makes a good try but gets in the hands of the wrong helper or otherwise does not make significant progress.

Occasionally I am told that I have a great store of patience with regard to clients. It doesn't seem to me to be patience at all, but rather a partial understanding of their difficulties. I continue to be amazed at the huge proportion of wives and husbands of alcohol troubled people who stick with it year after interminable year; I would have to say frankly that I simply wouldn't stay with such a person.

My instincts, my personality, my awareness of the fact that we have but one life available to us, and my experience with alcohol troubled people all persuade me to urge the unloading of such people after a reasonable period of attempting to be of help on the part of the spouse and children. I am convinced that the helper in the family must become informed about alcohol abuse and must face the problem intelligently, but at some point it is probably best for the alcohol-damaged person as well as the spouse and kids for the marriage to be terminated.

Why should Mary work harder at the problem than John, if John is the destructive drinker, the primary person? After ten years of no peace, no love, no security, too much physical and emotional pain, we must conclude that Mary herself is disturbed if she stays with him. Surprisingly, she probably hurts him in his efforts to quit by permitting his continued irrational behavior to affect her life.

The point is perhaps best illustrated by vignettes of two severely alcohol-damaged men and their wives and families. One did extremely well, and the other is still drinking sporadically and destructively.

Pat had been a confidant, speech-writer, and high officeholder in politics. The governor of the state at one time could pick up the phone and ask Pat for a speech on, say, urban renewal. Pat would grind out a politically savvy speech for the governor to use, sight unseen but safely, the next day.

Pat had seven kids, one of whom had cystic fibrosis and

could not be expected to live very long, and a long-suffering wife, Marie, who found herself unable to stem the rising tide of Pat's heavy drinking. Her husband was no longer home very much, and when he was he was too absorbed in himself and his flakiness to relate to her and the children. He was admitted several times to a hospital that had a psychiatric unit. By the third admission he was out of work, grossly depressed and frightened, and somatically preoccupied; he kept looking at his face and body in the mirror and was desperately concerned about his deteriorating physical condition and appearance.

On his sixth admission, now with an incorrect diagnosis of schizo-affective reaction, depressed type (he was pretty crazy by now) he was of no use to the family, providing neither financial nor emotional support. He constituted only a drain on Marie, who was now working and attempting to keep a dying child alive by frequent trips to a medical center fifty miles away.

On this admission Pat fell into the hands of a helper who spotted alcohol as the basic cause of the disorder. The helper called Marie at Pat's request and because wives should be involved in helping enterprises.

Marie had had it. She had obtained a restraining order to keep him out of the house, was about to finalize a legal separation (her religion prevented divorce), and wanted nothing further to do with Pat.

Over several weeks the helper squeezed out of Marie a tentative indication that Marie *might* let Pat see the kids if he went dry for a year, obtained employment, and contributed financially and emotionally to the family. In no mood to trifle further, she emphasized that all this was against her better judgment and that he would have to deliver *first*.

The short version of this true tale is that, despite false starts and a desperate struggle, Pat met her demands, began reintegrating himself into the family by attending his kids' birthday celebrations (it is probably fortunate that there were seven children!) and finally returned to his family.

On the day his son died, Pat was in the helper's office within three hours of the boy's death, dissolved in tears but carrying a kind of dignity about him, saying that he would be eternally grateful that he had been with the boy, as a proper father, for the child's last year and a half. They had fished, watched TV, read and talked, gone to the hospital together, and had even managed a thirteenth birthday for the boy.

Although Pat had certainly done his part, and the helper his, Marie's refusal to let him continue as he was in their family life was absolutely crucial. Although she loved him, she consciously risked his death in the gutter rather than let him poison everything for eight other people.

Jim, on the other hand, had a wife who was herself an "understanding," sympathetic, and sober member of AA. His mother had died of alcoholic cirrhosis, and neither Jim nor his prominent father had ever forgiven the physician for writing the true cause on the death certificate. Both parents not only overlooked Jim's alcoholic pecadilloes but encouraged them by giving him money for driving-while-intoxicated fines and by "fixing" other alcohol-related crimes for him.

Jim was very bright and verbal and managed to hang on to his teacher's job by virtue of those qualities, his father's "pull," and the fact that he could charm the birds out of the trees when he wanted to.

He had abandoned his first wife and their four kids; he drank in sprees and spent all his money and all the earnings of his second wife, Barbara, who worked. Barbara learned that when Jim was drinking he became a monster, beating her up viciously and repeatedly. When she began to leave him during these times, she always left hints or messages so that he could find her, beat her up, and destroy her apartment and clothing.

She kept making excuses for him, saying he was a really nice guy when sober (although he had about ten of these insane binges per year). On one occasion he was picked up by the state police and charged after he had "eloped" from a dry-out farm, gone to the nearest bar, and threatened to dynamite the place from which he had just escaped. His father pulled strings and Barbara moved heaven and earth to get the charges dropped.

She remains with him to this day. Both are basically unchanged, but miraculously both are still alive.

The family members are in a position to be the first to recognize a developing or crystalized alcohol problem, and they will generally feel the damaging effects before anyone else in the drinker's life. Very often, however, family members are not well enough informed, or are too defensive, or both, to run up the red warning flag when they ought to. The family, after all, is likely to share with the troubled member many of the same values toward alcohol usage. The problem most often develops subtly and insidiously in social settings and is very likely to be within subcultural norms.

Again, if the word *alcoholic* turns people's minds off and conjures up an inaccurate set of perceptions ("George doesn't get drunk very often" or "He only drinks beer" or "She doesn't drink every day, after all," and other useless notions) then the family members have been denied the opportunity to have the perceptions, hold the attitudes, and take the actions that could help.

Family members who can't help are a tragic waste of the best helpers available. If society in general misses the boat about what alcohol damage is, it is not surprising if the family members who make up the society also fail to make the needed connections. I believe we can lay that failure at the door of the words *alcoholic* and *alcoholism,* improperly defined and badly clarified.

The social area is, of course, much larger than the family. It includes neighbors, the PTA and the kids' teachers, one's employer or spouse's employer, employees, colleagues or co-workers; one's social friends or the children's friends, the members of one's religious group or bowling league, and so on. The possibilities of breakdown in any of these social relationships are enormous, of course.

Several years ago I was flown to a midwestern university by its administration to try to help a friend of the institution who appeared to be having problems with alcohol. He proved to be a pleasant, gregarious, self-made man in the construction business, earning an income well into six figures. He was also scared to death.

He had developed an informal and efficient system for handling his business. He himself was overall chief and contract-obtainer; his brother ordered and paid for materials; and a long-time employee who was also a friend and confidant scheduled the work and handled personnel.

About five weeks before I met with him and his wife, he had been brought up short by a series of upsetting incidents. He had grown increasingly suspicious of his brother because profits were falling off, and he had flown into an accusatory rage that he had felt to be justified at the time. The brothers were now estranged, and it appeared that the accusations might not be forgiven and that his brother might leave the company. When the owner had spoken to the confidant-employee, that individual had to his surprise taken the brother's side and had told the owner that the business was falling off because the owner was not doing *his* job. Always a heavy drinker, he had for the past six months been leaving work at ten each morning to play a round of golf. At one o'clock he was drinking, and twelve hours later, at one in the morning, he was getting home. Further, said the friend, he himself had been getting hollered at lately, and *he* wouldn't take much more of it.

The worst was yet to come.

This man had been very close to his wife for many years. She was warm, supportive, and affectionate. Now she was talking about serious difficulties in their relationship that made her desperately unhappy, and she was wondering how long she could stick.

He concluded, on the advice of all concerned, that he'd

better give up drinking for awhile. He became terror-stricken when he found he couldn't, because he had always considered himself master of his own fate. He was able to bring himself to confide in one of his friends at the university.

The upshot was that in two visits with him and his wife (one over dinner) the necessary adjustments occurred and have held for two years.

The story illustrates these points:

1. The fact that the wife had a good relationship with him and was concerned when it was threatened was extremely helpful. She was also a very quick learner and an unusually straight talker. (This relationship falls under the family sub-category.)
2. The strained relationship with his well-liked brother and his employee, who were also good straight talkers, helped.
3. The business was being damaged, which anticipates the next area, financial, and concern for the business helped clarify the situation.

This story also illustrates some principles that are taken up elsewhere in the book: (a) It is profitable to attack alcohol issues early; (b) there is real hope for people with alcohol problems; (c) we do have many ways and systems for helping successfully; and (d) it is time to count successes rather than defining as "alcoholic" the person who doesn't respond quickly, or at all, to attempts at repairing alcohol damage.

Again, the definition depends very firmly and simply *only* on the concept of *trouble* being associated with drinking.

The social area in our definition is huge in that it also covers fantasy relationships and avoidance of relationships. It has been said that alcoholism is a disorder of the lonely, which is probably accurate as far as it goes. It is also a difficulty endured by the frightened, the shy, the depressed, those who got in trouble through social drinking—but *all* of whom have consciously or unconsciously elected to reduce their anxiety by use of a mindbending chemical.

The social component in our definition is discussed with

an important goal in mind: Whether you are engaged in helping as a professional or as a family member, friend, or co-worker of someone who is possibly hurting from alcohol, you can make a valid judgment that alcohol troubles exist if the person you are concerned about is disturbing his relationships with other people because of drinking.

I have an old and valued friend who has always stood ready to help me if I should need it, and the arrangement is definitely bilateral. He is currently involved with a fine woman who is good for him and his child. In fact, he needs this person so much that he becomes frightened at the thought of losing her and can admit that comfortably and honestly to her and to me.

He likes his beer, and hard liquor now and then besides. He is a physical fitness buff, has never acquired an addiction to cigarettes, runs every day, and generally takes pretty good care of himself. He almost never gets drunk or even high, but he is an absolute son of a bitch when he's had alcohol, and he then calls his woman friend terrible things. Out of his need for her, he accuses her of doing the things he is most afraid she will do—and thus increases his likelihood of losing her.

As the three of us talked this over, she clearly described the situation—he never acts that way when he's not drinking. He has to stop, or at least cut back, and he knows that now, even though he had to make it clear that he's not an alcoholic because he doesn't get drunk. "No, but you're *different* when you drink," says the woman. She's right, and she is able to perceive the situation accurately when asked the uncomplicated, unembarrassing question, "Is drinking connected in any way to the troubles you're having?"

They never really thought of that before in any potentially helpful way, but they do now. And they were not driven into a long, embittering denial of an accusation, because no charges of "alcoholic" were ever leveled against him.

Some time ago a professional helper, Dr. Joan Jackson,

penned some admirable words with regard to the predictable form of the family's response to the alcohol troubled individual. Jackson's thinking was directed principally to professionals who deal with the wives of alcoholics—it is too bad that they have not been exposed in larger numbers to her ideas. To give her notions a fair hearing it is necessary to refer to an outgrowth of the Freudian psychoanalytic system, a system that is still ingrained in the heads of mental health professionals. (One often wonders why so many people continue to insist on using psychoanalysis with alcohol troubled people, since the great man himself made it clear that it would not work with alcoholics.)

In any event, a mix-up occurred, and through a misunderstanding, professionals came up with the following formulation:

Freud said that troubled, neurotic people are that way because it helps them survive. It follows logically in this system, if not in real life, that any woman neurotic enough to marry a man with alcohol troubles would necessarily require him to stay that way, or else her neurotic needs would no longer be met. He might, for example, become more adequate as a human being, and presumably she needs him to be either dependent on her or somehow one down.

The truth of this formulation was supposedly demonstrated by the fact that the wives of severely alcohol-damaged men are extremely mistrustful of the therapeutic progress being made. They even fail to turn the family financial accounts and checkbooks back to the husband after he has gone dry for a couple of weeks under the ministrations of his latest professional helper.

Jackson pointed out, however, clearly and concisely, that as the alcohol troubled husband deteriorates, he cumulatively destroys the trust and confidence his wife is able to place in him. She learns through repeated experience that she is unwise to let him handle the finances, since he burns the rent money in a barroom with the boys, and she understandably becomes extremely reluctant to let him have it back as he recovers.

Marie, mentioned earlier in this section, was one such. She fit Jackson's model exactly. She had been through the situation much more often than the helper—and she and her children had to face extremely serious consequences each time Pat failed to deliver.

The wife thus of necessity becomes the stabilizing head of the family, and she has learned that she *must* be a doubter. The husband *can* earn his way back, and he does in case after case. But, as Jackson puts it, the confidence has to be built up again just as it was eroded, piece by piece and sometimes over a fairly long period of time.

I earnestly urge helpers to refrain from taking sides against wives—just find a way to help, not to assign responsibility.

It is productive to deal with family units when at all possible, and the failure to do so is a shortcoming in the practices of many professional helpers. In addition, it would be extremely helpful if we could capitalize on an alcohol axiom—"The family is the first to know." (One might add, "Provided the members of the family are informed and educated.")

The U.S. government, through its National Institute for Alcohol Abuse and Alcoholism (NIAAA), a division of the sprawling Department of Health, Education and Welfare (HEW), has in the last few years mounted an exciting new system for identification and help for employed alcohol-involved people. In my opinion there have been some severe difficulties in the conceptualization and execution of the NIAAA programs: (1) a massively expensive but useless statistical and evaluation system; (2) an inability either to understand or to implement programs based on the principle that alcohol troubles should be dealt with early (the reporting system for funded programs asks how much beer, wine, hard liquor, and so on are consumed in thirty days); and (3) a difficulty in accepting the fact that one doesn't have to be "late stage" to warrant legitimate concern from the primary alcohol unit.

For example, a portion of the educational propaganda that went out for a while was the logo or symbol of "95," which very accurately and helpfully reminded us that 95 percent of people with alcohol difficulties are unidentified and therefore unhelped. Some grants were awarded for programs to deal with that fact. Subsequently, a subsection of NIAAA became unhappy that grantee agencies were dealing with other than skid-row bums and were in fact intervening early and even preventively (often successfully). The word began filtering back, "But this is alcoholism money, and you're not working exclusively with alcoholics."

And then the "95" logo disappeared from the promotional material.

Further, the reporting system provided no way to report the numbers of children and spouses of alcohol troubled people who were being seen and helped, both to help themselves and to help the "primary" person—another indication that NIAAA, or some of its personnel, were "late-stage"-oriented and not family-and-prevention-oriented.

On the other hand, the system was commendable in several respects: The "95 percent" notion had at least a brief life and wide exposure. Many agencies and people learned something for the first time about alcohol problems in the United States. And the fact that these programs were oriented around an occupational program indicated a solid effort to move toward earlier intervention.

The occupational programs were and are based on a very good idea—train people and agencies to go into business and industry to set up a referral system within plants and offices so that if an employee is functioning badly he can be referred to knowledgeable sources for a determination as to whether or not his problems are alcohol-based.

It is a clever idea and a sound one. It has already had a massive impact and is therefore highly desirable and commendable. But it is still a little late if the axiom "The family is the first to know" holds true.

Although these programs inject federal money into the social and financial components, they are leaving out the family, which means we're still too late.

To underline the importance of intervention at the family or social level, we can construct a ranked list of places in which the alcohol troubled individual can be identified, and of people who can identify him, in descending order of likelihood of identification. The first locations on the list are associated with the most damage and the alcohol troubled people there are easiest to notice. The later entries on the list are, at least logically, closer and closer to early involvement, and deal with people who have suffered less damage. They have a demonstrably higher "hit rate" for helping, and for helping more quickly and cheaply. Unfortunately, it is so far easier to spot a dead alcohol troubled person than a live one, and a severely damaged one is easier to spot than one who is minimally or moderately impaired. Even then, we do not identify with great accuracy even in the dead-and-dying categories.

In general, we can identify alcohol troubles in specific places in the following order, noting that in a sense the list is inverted—we identify best where we can help least, or less expeditiously:

1. *Morgues.*   Here we find, and can count, if we wish, dead drivers, drownings, fatal falls, suicides, people who expire in hospitals of cirrhosis, malnutrition, DTs, pneumonia, bleeding ulcers, and so forth.

2. *Emergency rooms and general hospital beds.*   Here we find the physically ill or physically traumatized who are not yet dead and who hopefully will not become so. These people are really hurting, however, and a number will, in fact, die.

3. *"Mental health" operations.* These are often not actually mental *health* facilities but mental *illness* ones, because they are usually places where people who are *already* emotionally troubled can get put back together. This is true of inpatient beds in specialty or "psychiatric" hospitals, out-patient treatment in community mental health clinics, and most private practitioners.

The mental health model is not very effective yet in early identification and prevention in *any* area within its purview, but it is strikingly weak in the alcohol area. We can demonstate very quickly that about half of outpatient clients have substantial alcohol troubles that are contributing to their difficulties in living. The same is true of inpatient clients, yet there is no general alertness and expertise in mental health facilities with regard to the problem.

It is encouraging, however, to note that awareness is found increasingly in the mental health field, even though there is still a great distance to go.

4. *Physicians' offices and practices.* Huge numbers of alcohol-involved individuals can be identified in these settings. I stress repeatedly that trained and alert physicians often do diagnose the alcohol difficulty and frequently solve the problem quickly and efficiently. We in alcohol work hear too much about the joker who cannot attend very well to his family physician or internist when he says, "George, your symptoms are related in large part to alcohol. If you want to feel better [or live more than six months] you'll have to cut back or give it up." We also know that astounding numbers of patients respond quickly, *even when in severe alcohol trouble.* Not everyone going down the chute with booze is ornery or crazy. Frequently the patient responds very reasonably with, "OK, Doc. I guess I have been overdoing it. I'll take a whack at it." And does.

5. *Health maintenance organization.* The HMO is po-

tentially a unique means of delivering health services. The general notion is that you prepay for health care services just as you do for, let us say, Blue Cross, but with a very important difference. Blue Cross simply pays somebody to take care of you after you're sick; the HMO in principle tries to keep you well, or at least to catch your problems early, because they lose money if they have to operate on you, or hospitalize you, or pay for some other expensive procedure that could have been prevented. So it doesn't cost you anything beyond your regular premium, for example, to go to the HMO when you have a moderate fever. They treat it right away and prevent an expensive pneumonia.

Some HMOs even divide up a pool of money among the employees at the end of the year if they have done a good job of keeping their members well enough not to drain the money out of the pool.

HMOs have many problems right now. Most of them are new and struggling financially, so they don't add more physicians until they absolutely have to, and a too-small staff can't do a very good job of prevention—they're running too fast keeping up with sick people. Medical organizations aren't too delighted with the system because it smacks of socialized medicine. It's not so lucrative and it makes the money-makers feel a bit guilty because keeping people well is a nicer idea than helping them only when they're sick.

So, although present HMOs frequently have a lot of troubles that reduce their ability to prevent and to identify early, they're a natural for an early identification and true prevention system for alcohol troubles. Think of the money they'd save, not just on the primary person with alcohol problems but also on children who don't get abused or malnourished, or wives who don't get depressed, for example. (Blue Cross is at last beginning to notice, too.)

The dream of the HMO concept, then—"Don't let them get sick"—can be realized better by diligently attending to alcohol awareness in HMO staffs. Because the central, ruling concept is prevention, early diagnosis, and treatment, I have placed HMOs farther down the list than the "fix 'em when they're sick" components of the system. Ideally, HMOs ought to catch problems at a less severe level.

6. *Clergy, social workers, public health nurses, police.* These people have excellent vantage points from which to identify developing alcohol problems a good deal earlier than those in the previous categories, because they do not have to wait for the alcohol disorder to be so severe and chronic that massive physical or emotional breakdown has occurred. They are often, but by no means always, alerted by members of the family or by an acquaintance:

"I'm worried about Joe, Father. He's spending a lot of time down at the Silver Tap lately."

Or, "That's the third time this month you've driven Buddy home, Sergeant. What gives with him?"

7. *Employers and teachers.* Potentially employers and teachers have opportunities to spot moderate (as well as more severe) alcohol troubles about as soon and often as the people in the previous group. Employers and teachers must be alerted through education and training seminars to notice trouble or poor performance in the troubled person. They are *not* usually well advised to attempt to solve the problem themselves but should get the individual to knowledgeable helpers or helping agencies.

A good friend of mine suggests to employers that when employees start spoiling "widgets," or whatever is being produced on the assembly line, it's time to look.

Corporations and big banks bring along vice-presidents for years, grooming them for the top job, only to lose them to booze. Better to respond to the failing performance and make it a condition of retaining the job to get help.

You will note that when the NIAAA funded programs

to go after problems in item 7 they came pretty far down the list. That is a major accomplishment.

The cold fact is, however, that if the problem is first noticed by the relative outsiders in categories 1 through 7, it is a pretty bad problem already. Most of us are on our best behavior out of the house, and you have to have a rather large booze problem to shake enough to spoil whatever widgets you make for a living.

So we must find ways to get to category 8, families ("the first to know"), and to 9, the alcohol troubled person himself or herself. There is *no* way to do this short of broad-scale, accurate education on *facts* and *feelings* about alcohol. In this regard, academic courses on alcohol are lovely because they (a) draw to them people who have a personal or family concern and (b) give them enough factual material and emotional clarity to be able to ponder the issues usefully. It's almost as good for a member of the family to know something about it as for the individual involved to notice it. I am convinced that widespread dissemination of just a few helpful facts, attitudes, and techniques would vastly increase early family referrals and self-referrals and would increase the hit rate by saving an average of five years' destructive drinking.

That is the difference between categories 8 and 9 versus 1 through 7—about five years on the average.

This discussion has several themes—each category has some people who spot the troubles, but in each one probably most do not. Even in morgues, for example, it's clear that blood alcohol level is rarely taken in drowning cases. Most wives wouldn't know a minimal or moderate alcohol problem if they slept with one. Yet each category is a good candidate for utilizing alcohol information if and as we alert people more widely and accurately.

I teach a course on the alcohol troubled person that draws large numbers of professionals. About a year ago, halfway through the course, an industrial nurse, employed by a large utility whose employees have their share of alcohol troubles, told a story in class. She was angry about the human waste, and the course was helping her sort out her feelings and was giving her information she had never had, and we had just finished talking about the foregoing categories. We used her story in class for a very productive discussion, and I asked her to write it down for inclusion in my book:

"One of my neighbors, approximate age late fifties or early sixties, had not worked for several years due to poor health. He suddenly developed convulsions and was admitted to the hospital via the emergency room. He died after several days in the hospital.

"His family was quite upset and angered when they were informed he died because of DTs. The family really could not believe this because he did all of his drinking at home, drank only beer, and retired early each night. True enough, he was a constant daily drinker—but never drunk."

The better we inform, the more prevention and early identification we can accomplish. And checking the social area for indications of alcohol-related trouble is productive in assisting us to understand and identify the issues early.

Financial Components

The financial aspect of alcohol troubles includes, but is not confined to, one's job. A practical rule of thumb about the financial area is to figure out whether the individual in question is drinking at least ten or fifteen dollars' worth of alcohol a week. If so, there is a high risk of getting into trouble or of already being there. Note that it is merely an *alerting* rule of thumb, *not* a statement of actual trouble. Our definition in the last analysis requires the presence of troubles.

When checking this one out, by the way, be careful not to be taken in by the argument that a person is not actually spending that much money. The rule says ten or fifteen dollars' worth—we aren't concerned about who he cons free drinks out of or how.

It is useful on occasion to reduce the dollar value of alcohol consumed to a percentage of take-home pay. For example, suppose individual X makes $10,400 per year and drinks twenty dollars' worth a week, a trick that is not so difficult in today's market. Since he makes $200 per week, he is drinking 10 percent of his gross. Depending on number of dependents and so forth, Internal Revenue and Social Security may reduce his take-home pay to about $160 or even less, in which case he's devoting almost 13 percent of take-home pay to his "social drinking."

That's a hefty tax, or a pretty good investment. Spending this amount on alcohol represents trouble if the person has never been able to buy a house because he can't scratch up the money. He's spending on alcohol $87 per month that could go toward a mortgage. This guy has troubles if he can't meet his bills or pay his kids' tuition or buy them clothes.

It may be helpful to him to interpret a cessation of drinking as a twenty-dollar-a-week raise (or twenty-five before taxes) in addition to all its other benefits.

Again I insert a note of caution, because if his income is $50,000 a year, or maybe even $20,000, twenty dollars a week will not by itself cause trouble. If, on the other hand, his drinking reduces his on-the-job efficiency so that he gets passed over for a promotion otherwise quite within his capabilities, we should take that into account as we decide whether or not alcohol troubles exist.

Of course, we must readily rule alcohol *out* as a troubling agent when our definition helps us do so; we are *never* trying to assign troubles to drinking if that is not realistic —we are simply trying to assess the situation honestly.

In continuing our examination of the financial aspect of the definition we are constantly reminded that the in-

vestigation is situation-specific, so the individual's life circumstances must be considered as a whole to help us locate
(or rule out) troubles.

Suppose Henry owns a factory and has excellent man-
agers, policy-makers, and quality-control employees. If he
drinks heavily over the weekend and cannot come to work
on Monday he does not suffer financially, because his income continues at its usual level. Presume, too, that even
if his judgment is negatively affected, his managerial staff
provides him adequate protection. Henry does not at this
time fall under our definition of alcohol problems *in the
financial area*, although he may do so socially, physically,
or emotionally.

Working in Henry's factory is an employee, Ken, who
over the same weekend drank about the same way as his
employer did, or maybe even a good deal less. If he cannot
make it to work on Monday, however, his week's income
is reduced by at least a fifth, if you'll pardon the expression,
even without considering his possible loss of lucrative over-
time. He also risks being pegged by Personnel as unreliable
or too sickly to retain or promote—a decision that can
bring a career to a standstill without the employee's knowledge. If Ken somehow drags himself into the place but, due
to depression, a big head, irritability, shakiness, or concern
over his wife's unhappiness with him, does not turn out his
quota of widgets or doesn't make them well he is in further
jeopardy.

Henry and Ken exemplify the situation-specific aspect
of our definition; Ken is in significant financial trouble with
alcohol and Henry is not. We have determined accurately
and quickly and without creating hard feelings in Ken that
he has troubles. Those troubles may become grimmer with
time and they may not, but right now he's got them, and
right now is the time for him to get help, even if that help
consists only in demonstrating to him what is happening.
Ken may not even know what he's doing to himself because

he believes he shows none of the "classical" signs of the
"alcoholic." For example, he never drinks alone, can go for
days without any, and so on.

The situation-specific definition—which defines some
people as troubled and some as untroubled even if they
drink at the same rate—is hard for many people to accept
at first. It is easier to blame someone or something else for
the problem, but the guidelines are clear and straightforward—trouble is trouble, whatever the details.

It may be helpful to examine the financial category
along several dimensions: income, outgo, and chronological
finances.

Income.   Income criteria include whether one has and
keeps a job, whether investments are sound and timely,
whether raises come when expected, whether earning time
is lost, and so forth. Maybe an individual, for example, is
essentially retired after having "made it" but is too befuddled with genteel drinking to exercise his stock options
or sell his rights before they expire. Maybe the poor fellow's
hands shake too much to clip his coupons. If so, he's damaging his income.

Outgo.   Another aspect of the financial area of our definition is the way income gets spent and whether or not options and freedom of outgo are lost through drinking.

One of my colleagues in the alcohol-education enterprise got caught in both the income and outgo squeeze.
Since he is one of my unofficial repairers-of-manuscripts he
will have read this and sanitized it for complete accuracy
by the time it reaches you.

His father was a highly competent professional man
who by virtue of that fact amassed a considerable sum of
money that he was unable to bequeath in the usual way
to his son, because the latter was at that time an unstable
drunk. The father quite wisely and considerately tied up

the goodly estate in a trust so his grown offspring would not blow it.

Now my friend James is stable and sober and reliable indeed, having found AA and other noble endeavors. Although now absolutely capable, he lives partially off the income of the trust and must, by its terms, go through an executor to get to the restricted and guarded principal.

He has lost important income and outgo options.

Most of us buy automobile tires when they go on sale if we can. We worry about getting the most out of our shrinking dollar. Some of us can easily afford twenty dollars a week for alcohol, but the majority can't, and to many Americans a regular drain of five dollars a week or less for alcohol is significant.

The outgo dollar is affected in ways other than simply whether we can afford to divert money into the actual purchase of alcohol or into being a free-spending macho big shot in the local pub or country club.

Troubles tend to pile on troubles. When a person has an auto accident, his insurance rate goes up or he finds he can't get insurance anymore. Since the person in trouble with alcohol is capable of letting a lot of things slide, he may let car maintenance go because he's short of cash or morale or discipline, and that increases his statistical chances of suffering a blowout or brake failure. Soon he totals the car, which he needs to get to work, and he doesn't have insurance. He has to pay extra medical bills to get his forehead stitched, and he loses another day from work.

You may not be aware that if you knock down a telephone pole you own it—you buy another one from the utility company and bear the expense of having it installed. I know a guy who bought several of them in his home town —they're expensive and also tend to wrinkle your car. Such expenses constitute a part of the outgo problem.

One accident is probably just an accident, but a couple of them indicate trouble that can be avoided.

Driving is only one aspect of outgo problems, of course. Other obvious areas stem from running harder because everything is beginning to go wrong—shoring up faltering self-esteem by throwing bigger parties, buying a new dress, or generally flinging around a diminishing store of cash to prove you have plenty of money when you haven't.

It is amazing to note the multitude of ways in which financial troubles are related to alcohol use; human ingenuity in this regard is almost inexhaustible.

Chronological Finances

To understand financial issues, it is helpful not only to think in terms of income and outgo but also to overcome any tendency to think only in the present. We need to consider the past—it can be overcome in the financial area as well as in others, certainly, but past drinking-related financial problems and lost opportunities affect the present, and the future will certainly be related to what happens today.

A lawyer friend of mine who is a long-term and successful member of AA once told me about an incident from his drinking days. He was laying in a good supply in a hotel bar on Rhode Island's charming Block Island. He progressed from good fellowship through conviviality to philosophy, and from there to how the hotel bar could be improved, on his inexorable way to oblivion. Somewhere between conviviality and philosophy he was joined by the hotel's owner, who drew on his reserves of strength and fortitude to match my friend drink for drink. At the bar-improvement stage the owner suggested that if my friend could do better he ought to buy the place, and they signed initial agreement papers right there on the polished mahogany. When Joe recovered from his oblivion stage he found the agreement in his pocket. The price was advantageous but he backed out because he was not in good financial shape due to his repeated convivialities and he did not trust his judgment on matters sealed under the influence of Demon Rum.

He should have made an exception on that one.

In the alcohol field, one increasingly finds individuals who have made what appears to be a poor trade. Having been through the ravages of alcohol and usually having reached the severe level of damage, these people may give up the work they were trained to do in order to become alcohol helpers. Some do well for themselves financially and emotionally by going this route, and through the infusion of their personal experience and dedication the field is improving. Many of them have made, and are making, excellent contributions.

On the other hand, substantial numbers of these people are either not temperamentally suited, or not broadly enough trained and informed, to be of long-term benefit to others. Many are narrow-based "teachers" about alcoholism rather than continuing to be learners as well as teachers. Through an odd alchemy the personal experience of having handled alcohol badly has become in some circles an honored badge of the expert. That particular personal experience makes a good helper or program developer *only* when coupled with an ability to rise above one's own experience *and* an ability to learn more.

The person who does not rise above his own specific life circumstances is exemplified by the man, once severely alcohol-damaged, who appeared on an educational television program as a member of a panel beamed at thousands of people in an effort to alert viewers to early problems with alcohol. With an air of certainty, he asserted that "nobody is an alcoholic unless he drinks before breakfast. I know, because that's what I did."

He obviously had his own idiosyncratic definition of the problem. The remainder of the panel spent the rest of the program attempting to correct his absurdity, which nevertheless must have provoked at least some ATPs to turn to their wives and say, "See? I don't have a problem with alcohol. Now stay off my back."

Whether or not the recovering alcohol troubled person is this self-centered, it would appear wise at least at first for the recovering person to regard the helper's role as a temporary one, to be utilized only as a means to return to his or her former occupation, at which many were excellent. If one proves during this interlude to have skills in the area and *if it promotes real personal growth,* then a second decision might later be made to stay in it.

The alcohol helper's role is being used by increasing numbers of people to avoid going back to their careers and competing. When used in this way it is simply a continuation of the destructive loss of self-confidence suffered during the drinking. It is not helpful, for example, for the individual who was a $25,000-a-year executive to hole up as an $8,500-a-year alcohol counselor just because he's had "all that experience as an alcoholic" or to be an unpaid community crusader for the cause while unemployed. He can do better work for more people by using his good mind to rise in the company to a policy-making position and helping alcohol troubled people from within the company or as an avocation. He will not then have sold himself and his family short by continuing the financial troubles that started during the active drinking period.

On the other hand, many people who have been alcohol troubled find that as they overcome their difficulties they are happier and more productive than at any time in their lives. For those who were modestly paid because they were once not using their full potential and who subsequently become solid citizens, there is excellent reason to try the alcohol helper route. Good, useful jobs exist in the field, and the man or woman who has had the problem is proving to be constructive, providing he or she is not running away, that he comprehends that there are experiences more inclusive than his own, that he has a real knack for the work, and that he can think "learner" as well as "teacher."

Under these conditions the financial and personal losses sustained in the past need not be continued in the present and projected into the future.

Physical Components

By the time measurable or visible physical damage is evident, it is usually clear that we are dealing with either a moderate or a severe instance of alcohol trouble. Although the four areas in our definition must be separated for purposes of discussion, they do not, of course, fall neatly into discrete bundles in real life, and it is essential to think of them as interlocked and interacting areas. If one has a significant problem in, let us say, the social area, it will almost certainly be reflected in, let us also say, the emotional area.

I have separated the physical area from the emotional in order to present a more meaningful discussion. These two areas are really more tightly interlocked and overlapping than the others, and the reader should remain constantly alert to this fact.

A very reasonable definition of *emotion* suggests that an emotion is something that you *feel,* and a person cannot feel in the absence of physical change. If the body does not make a physiological adjustment, one simply cannot be having an emotion. Heartbeat is one easy way to measure the presence of an emotion. It may speed up, slow down, get stronger or weaker, skip a beat or become quite erratic and arrhythmic. Blood pressure is another measure. It too can go up or down, slightly or sharply, or can vary. Emotion generates perspiration, as measured by the psychogalvanic skin response (when the skin has a film of perspiration, it conducts electricity better).

Emotion can affect breathing rate, volume of air exchanged with each breath, and regularity of breathing.

Emotion can alter the chemical bath in which the brain and the rest of the body functions, since under strong or repeated emotion the body burns up sugar faster, has an increased adrenalin output, sweats off salts, and so forth. Necessarily, then, the electrical control center, or brain, fires at different rates and intensities, bringing about a change in thinking.

Blood is sent to different locations for different emotions under varied levels of pressure.

Under the influence of emotion, digestive and excretory functions can be altered—some people are unable to retain sphincter control under the impact of a sudden, large stimulus input of fear, such as a near miss on the highway.

And obviously sexual feelings (emotions) produce physiological changes.

We cannot, then, have an emotion without undergoing at least a temporary, and sometimes under chronic emotion permanent, physical change. Conversely, we do not endure physical change (pain, teen-age pimples, increase in height or weight, falling or graying hair, loss of organ or limb function, loss of teeth) without an emotional concomitant.

Often we do not sense or in any way become *aware* or conscious of our emotions; many well-known medical and psychological ills occur without the victim's awareness of a causative emotion.

Emotions (and thus physical change) can be triggered either subtly (as by a not-quite-recognized perfume from thirty years ago) or quite stunningly (as by the sight of blood or the sudden realization that your mother wasn't all that bad and you miss her).

Recall the headache you get at income tax time or when your husband hollers at you, the loss (or gain) in appetite when you're terribly happy and excited, or when you're frightened by the speech you foolishly agreed to make next week. When the trailer truck skids within inches of you in the snow at 60 m.p.h., what is your pattern? Immediate or delayed? Faint in the head? Or does your stomach "drop" or "turn over"? Or are your knees suddenly weak? Perhaps you fetch up with a migraine, or simply feel the sweat trickling down your sides, or have diarrhea.

Emotion and physical effects go together.

An extraordinarily wide range of physical disorders is intimately related to alcohol intake and nutritional deficit. Some, like alcoholic cirrhosis, continue to generate controversy as to the extent to which the disorder could be avoided if only the individual could eat or could utilize physiologically what he or she ate. Some of the physical disorders most directly linked to nutritional alcohol problems via avitaminosis are alcoholic cirrhosis of the liver, peripheral neuropathy, gastritis, ulcers, diabetes, tuberculosis, delirium tremens, two major brain syndromes (Korsakoff's Psychosis and Wernicke's Disease), epilepsy or seizure disorders, and blackouts. I will discuss each briefly, knowing that my coverage is cursory and intended to serve principally as a survey. Further, it should be understood that these disorders overlap into other areas that will be dealt with outside the nutritional area. Many other disorders definitely have nutritional aspects, although they are not as direct as in the foregoing disorders.

Avitaminosis

Avitaminosis is a general term indicating a lack of vitamin intake and/or utilization, with particular reference for our purposes to loss of brain function, including the functions of locomotion and balance. Heavy users of alcohol can look severely intoxicated even when they're not—staggering down the street or bouncing from wall to wall in the hospital corridor. It has been my experience that such severely damaged alcohol users simply don't like their green leafy vegetables and never did follow their mothers' advice to eat their spinach—and that, believe it or not, is important. The tendency not to eat balanced meals because one doesn't really like them and never has, combined with an alcohol-induced malfunctioning of the digestive system, puts reasonably heavy drinkers at double hazard.

Avitaminosis is a disorder to which any heavy drinker is vulnerable, but at special risk are people living alone or becoming solitary (and not sharing mealtimes) within a family. Persons living alone, particularly if things in their lives are not going well, may suffer from poor morale and depression. They tend to lack facilities for preparing nutritionally balanced meals, and as a consequence of their low morale, they do not take the trouble to eat well. Often they eat out, when they eat, and they tend to be meat-and-potatoes people. Rooming house districts churn out avitaminotic individuals at a high rate, but it is a mistake to assume that the suburban drinker, still living with his or her family, gets adequate nutrition. He or she may not like the foods necessary for good health, may suffer a declining appetite, and cannot fully utilize ingested food anyway.

A man in his fifties retired after a career that was successful but included heavy drinking. He had enough income to live in a nice apartment house, but he ate out at a local restaurant for its social value and because it had excellent food at reasonable prices. The waitresses understood that he wanted them to "hold the vegetables"—he wanted more meat, potatoes, and gravy instead. He ate every meal and always had dessert.

One day he lost his balance, fell off the stool, and was hospitalized with an avitaminotic brain.

Alcohol-involved people often require therapeutic doses of the vitamin B family during recovery. Nutrition must *always* be attended to in alcohol troubles. This is not a book on nutrition, but no responsible alcohol worker can afford to disregard it, since so many alcohol-associated disorders are *strongly* linked with nutritional deficit.

For basic information about vitamin and broader nutritional issues I suggest a quick glance at an encyclopedia under "vitamins." In any event, the ATP has traditionally had extra troubles maintaining proper nourishment.

Avitaminosis and the brain damage with which it can be associated is, like other physical damage, generally or usually reversible when the first signs occur and not as repairable later on.

Cirrhosis of the Liver

Laennec's, or alcoholic, cirrhosis of the liver occurs after reasonably chronic and heavy drinking, usually with nutritional deficit. The deficit *can occur even though the cirrhotic has been eating reasonably well*, because under some drinking conditions the digestive system cannot extract needed nutriment from the food. Many cirrhotics, of course, are *not* eating well.

Not all cirrhosis of the liver is caused by alcohol, but the figure is probably higher than 80 percent.

The liver can be regarded as a screen or filter that purifies the blood. Although the liver has many varied and vital functions, we will deal only with this filtering one. As the alcohol damage occurs, fatty deposits and scar tissue are built up in the liver, so that the physician can feel it becoming enlarged. To feel your liver he should have to press up under your bottom rib. If you have an enlarged, cirrhotic, fatty liver, his notes on your chart will say that he could feel the mass of your liver one, two, three, or four fingers below that rib. That's finger widths, horizontally. (You know, the way you order scotch.)

Let's use an example to demonstrate the screening function of the liver. Imagine that you open a can of paint that you partially used last fall. There is a skin on it by now, and if you wish to remove it properly you may get an old piece of window screen, place it over a bucket, and pour the paint through the screen to strain the lumps out of it. You have to pour slowly, because the screen will rapidly clog with impurities and will no longer filter. It backs up and overflows, so you have to get another piece of screening or shake out the original.

It's not so easy to replace a liver that is plugged up with fatty deposits and scarring, even though it would be nice to be able to after it stops filtering and permitting blood to go through easily. The result, of course, is that impure blood remains in the system, carrying incomplete metabolic products (toxic materials) to the brain. The individual therefore thinks badly, is confused, and has poor memory and judgment. He also may have poor balance or equilibrium. Often people with cirrhosis have jaundice, which is usually most easily seen in a distinct yellowing of the eyeballs and also of the skin in Caucasians.

Sometimes the backup pressure causes a swelling of the blood vessels in the esophagus, just as an innertube swells at a weak point under pressure. Such a swelling is an esophogeal varix, and sometimes varices break, creating a bloody mess and a life-threatening emergency, such as drowning in one's own blood or bleeding to death. Alcohol-damaged people should be checked for the presence of these unpleasant and dangerous manifestations of physical troubles more often than the average person.

Sometimes the pressure can be relieved only by a surgical procedure called a porto-caval shunt, in which a blood vessel is shifted to reroute, or shunt, some of the blood around the liver. That procedure obviously doesn't solve the impure blood problem, though.

Another manifestation of liver dysfunction is seen in the characteristic spider angioma, a small (as big as your little fingernail, maybe) pattern of red, octopus-shaped broken blood vessels very close to the surface of the skin. They may or may not be present on the face, but can often be seen on the shoulders and back, but usually higher than the waist, in a configuration that would be hidden by a T-shirt.

Sometimes associated with these liver, or hepatic, problems are "liver palms," palms that are too pale in the center and too red at the outer edges.

Ascites, or swelling of the belly caused by fluid retention, is another symptom of the cirrhotic liver and, like many other physical alcohol symptoms, is easily visible to the trained and alert eye. Many stigmata of the severely alcohol-damaged person are *highly* visible and provide readily available signposts for the helper. A damaged liver, of course, must be treated by a physician, but it doesn't take a physician's training to notice a swollen belly or yellowing eyeballs.

The ascitic belly is most visible on a skinny or even malnourished individual, in which case it looks like the belly of a starving child in India or Biafra. Ascites can occur, certainly, in heavier people. A "beer belly" may not be a beer belly in the popular, you're-getting-fat-because-you're-drinking-a-lot-of-beer sense.

Should the pressure build up too much, the physician may have to use a trocar, a hollow tube inserted into the fluid, to drain it, in which case it comes spurting out, driven by the pressure behind it. It may or may not interest you to know that navels have been known to burst under this pressure, permitting a stream about as thick as a pencil to shoot six to ten feet across the room.

I need to digress briefly at this juncture: Although one should not be averse to using "scare" tactics if necessary, such tactics work less often than helpers seem to think, if one can judge from the ease and regularity with which they resort to such bullying and overstated techniques. On the other hand, affected individuals or those who may become affected by drinking have a right to know what the simple facts are. Some of these facts are unpleasant and a bit gory —my intent is not to be more colorful than necessary but to be descriptive and informative.

I have alluded elsewhere to the necessity for mental health and medical professionals to learn more about alcohol, and I have referred specifically to the psychologist who never learned his alcoholism with regard to the ascites issue.

The story goes like this: In a staff conference in a mental health clinic the case of a young woman in treat-

ment for depression was being discussed. The situation of
the young woman's father was contributing to her depression, and in discussion some alcohol-alert staff members
began asking about the father's alcohol pattern. It became
evident that he was alcohol troubled and that this was
affecting the client. Her mother, who had been seen several
times about five years before by the psychologist in question, had in fact died several years before from alcohol-
related causes. (She had sat in a drunken stupor in the
rain, had caught pneumonia and, it turned out subsequently, had extreme liver damage that contributed to her
inability to recover.) The young woman nurtured an understandable love-hate ambivalence toward her now-dead
mother, who had been a very decent and competent person
in many ways. The daughter felt guilt, anger, and love all
mixed up together and contributing strongly to her significant depression.

The psychologist in question was characteristically
driven to turn every discussion toward a psychoanalytic,
psychodynamic formulation, but in this case, before he did
that, he opined, "Oh, I remember her mother. She had a
tumor or something in her belly when I was seeing her."

That was gross incompetence. The woman had cirrhotic
ascites, and alcohol was what killed her, and this man
believed and believes that you can't help "alcoholics" and
had said so in this case. Well, he couldn't and he can't yet,
and he won't and can't listen because he'll be a psycho-
dynamically oriented "therapist" until he dies or undergoes
a mystical conversion. There were in that room at least four
people who were alcohol-alert and knew what had happened
to the woman. No one spoke, for all had tried to show him
innumerable times in the past, and we all felt that once
again we would get as far as one would get attempting to
instruct a two-year-old in the basics of plane geometry.

People die at a great rate of alcoholic cirrhosis of the
liver. At one time I worked in a 370-bed general medical
hospital for adults, mostly males. The hospital buried about

two people per week from alcoholic cirrhosis. I guess that's not many in one sense, since it's only a hundred or so a year. On the other hand, if one were to stack them in a room it would be pretty full, or if one laid them end to end, head to foot, they would stretch about two hundred yards.

The last time I looked at our state Department of Health annual vital statistics, the fourth leading cause of death in males forty-five to sixty-four was alcoholic cirrhosis of the liver. This statistic is amazing when one realizes that in a very high proportion of cases the true cause of death does not find its way onto the death certificate, since it is a bit unpopular for the physician to call the shot straight—relatives tend to want to hide it. (The importance of cirrhotic deaths is also emphasized by the fact that the now little-used "Jellinek formula" for estimating prevalence of alcohol troubles in a given population used cirrhotic deaths as one variable.) Further militating against a compilation of true statistics is the fact that only recently are hospitals beginning even to *permit* admission with a primary diagnosis of alcoholism, so that the noncounting of cirrhosis has been part of a general conspiracy of silence and lack of awareness.

There is *no* way to avoid a conclusion of severe alcohol problems once a person shows signs of alcohol-related cirrhotic liver damage or other hepatic insufficiency. The body does not change that much, in that potentially fatal way, unless one has a terrible problem.

On the other hand, in this sector, as in other areas of alcohol problems, there are great and surprising latitudes and opportunities for second chances. The liver, if helped and supported properly and soon enough (and that can sometimes be amazingly late), has almost magical powers of recovery. For recuperation, however, it needs rest, adequate food, and no more alcohol. Given this set of circumstances the liver can often reconstitute itself. The body can absorb the fatty tissue; the filter can then start to work again; and the blood can clear up to permit the confused brain to put two and two together. Liver function tests will reflect the improvement (it may take weeks or months), and the physician will no longer be able to feel the liver below the rib. The yellow goes away, the spider angiomas recede, and the ascites disappears.

This is not to say you can continue to drink for a while after your symptoms have told someone your liver's in trouble, for the fact is that almost all the people who die of cirrhosis have been warned beforehand. The liver can be surprising in the extent to which it will forgive you, but it is also unpredictable about when it will shut down, once damaged.

The barroom folklore is filled with examples of Joe Schlunk having been told by a physician that if he didn't stop drinking he'd be dead in six months, and here's old Joe, three years later, still alive and still buying for the boys. Some professionals might have put it that way, but in my experience they're more likely to say something like, "Your liver is damaged and cannot heal itself until you stop drinking and start taking better care of yourself, including getting proper rest and nutrition. If you don't, you could be dead in six months, or you could possibly make it for longer."

Part of the problem with the severely damaged liver is that people's brains don't work very well when mud instead of oxygen gets pumped through them. I remember a nice guy named Arthur who was on my alcohol unit. He was of Portuguese descent, which is important to the story because of the closeness of family ties in that subculture, and he had drunk himself into cirrhosis, lost income, lost family—the whole bit. He arrived at the hospital in an ambulance, having endured one of those helicopter-plane-ambulance journeys from his island home, had progressed from medically critical to an OK-for-now-but-his-liver-studies-have-stopped-improving stage, and had been transferred to our unit still half-sick, half-yellow, and three-quarters confused. He cooperated completely, attended all meetings, became a regular AA member (but couldn't figure out why), and in general, except when too confused, did everything asked of him. Nobody and nothing on the unit could get through to him that he couldn't drink any more after he left, although he could somehow understand that he wasn't to drink while he was in the hospital.

The time limit on the unit was three months. I renewed him four times and finally got caught by the hospital director after Arthur had been there about a year. He was showing some signs of clearing up intellectually and I kept thinking, "He'll get it through his cirrhotic head any day now."

But he didn't. By now I had been ordered to discharge him. I asked his brother to come off the island to talk to me on the day Arthur was to leave. The brother listened to the problem and said very simply, "Arthur, the doctor says you can't drink anymore because you have an alcohol problem. You can't see my kids anymore if you drink."

A light of comprehension came into his eyes, and Arthur said, "Oh, I get it. OK."

It was as if he were saying, "Oh, for heaven's sake, why didn't you say so?"

For four years that I know of, he never again drank or was hospitalized. I got cards of thanks regularly from him and two invitations to visit the island during the tourist season.

Whatever else his brother did that I wasn't smart enough to do, I am certain he did it to a brain that was finally clearing from cirrhotic malfunctioning.

The literature reveals disagreements about whether alcoholic cirrhosis of the liver can occur in people who eat well while they drink. In practical terms, it is clear indeed that alcohol is related to the disorder and that nutrition probably is in most, if not all, cases. The problem is complicated by the fact that as alcohol intake becomes relatively heavy and/or chronic, at least two things happen: (1) the drinker's appetite may fall off, partly due to the fact that alcohol contains calories but no vitamins; (2) whatever food is eaten is not digested and utilized efficiently by the damaged body, so a person who is eating reasonably well may nevertheless suffer from malnutrition.

Peripheral Neuropathy

Peripheral neuropathy translates to damage, sometimes irreversible, to the nerves that serve the outlying regions of the body, principally the feet and legs. It is distinct from central nervous system damage such as the chronic brain disorders. The nerves can be compared to wires that carry electrical impulses by which we direct our limbs to lift, walk, or move (motor functions) or by which we feel warmth or cold, pressure, and so on (sensory functions). A sick nerve cell cannot deliver proper nutrition to the entire length of the nerve "wire." Since these nerves are quite long in the legs, they are more quickly damaged by poor nutrition there than in the arms and central areas of the body.

It is *not* logically possible to have peripheral neuropathy related to alcohol usage and simultaneously to deny severe ("late-stage") alcohol involvement, although many ATPs will maintain that position.

I recall a thirty-two-year-old house painter who had been in a wheelchair for seven months and would probably walk again but never climb a ladder, who maintained that his problem had nothing to do with his drinking (which happened to be "only" beer in horrendous quantities).

Peripheral neuropathy is signaled first by pain in the foot and lower leg, often accompanied by tingling and "pins and needles," and the lower extremities don't function as crisply and strongly as before. The sensations occur progressively higher in the long nerves as the alcohol/nutrition problem continues. Eventually there is pain, anesthesia, loss of muscle tone and muscle bulk, and the inability of the damaged nerves to carry "walk," "move," or "feel" messages.

Curiously, people seem to die or stop drinking, or something, before a great deal of arm neuropathy occurs.

The individual who has sustained heavy damage in this way is unlikely to be able to dance or climb stairs again with ease, if at all. Ambrose Barry, noted in the Dedication, had trouble with both until the end of his days. The condition is often accompanied by a "foot drop" (inability to pull the toes or foot up). People with peripheral neuropathy may have to go up stairs one step at a time (lift, place both feet on the same step, lift again).

Peripheral nerve damage is both painful and crippling. As in cirrhosis, the early signs serve as a timely warning that one is in *serious* alcohol trouble, but usually a quick response and correction can eliminate most of the symptoms.

The cure, as for cirrhosis, is rest, special attention to nutrition, especially the vitamin B group, and cessation of alcohol ingestion. Again, if this condition goes too far the body will no longer forgive, even if it does tend to show great latitude in these matters.

Gastritis and Ulcer

Gastritis is an inflammation of the sensitive mucosal lining of the stomach. The inflammation can be severe enough to result in bleeding, in which case material that is coughed up may have a "coffee-grounds" or dark-specked appearance, because the blood is not fresh by the time it gets out via that long route. Alcohol increases gastric acidity and therefore increases the chances of suffering gastritis.

Ulcers are simply sores, which in the digestive tract can erupt into bleeding sores. Obviously gastritis and ulcers are related—if you get the first from alcohol causes, you have set up conditions that can lead to the second.

Ulcers must sometimes be treated with a subtotal gastrectomy, an operation in which a portion of the stomach is removed or cut off because it has an ulcer that will not heal under less heroic measures, such as proper diet and reduction of psychic, or emotional, pressure. Vagotomy, or a cutting of a nerve, may also be necessary. Much too frequently people undergo gastrectomies because the surgeon cannot be bothered, or does not know enough, to diagnose an alcohol component in the etiology, or cause, of the ulcer. Such a procedure, when undertaken in a nonemergency situation and without learning the history and attempting to remove the contributory cause of alcohol intake, is incompetent and criminal. The patient is left with one-third, or three-quarters, or half of a stomach. Into this reduced area he continues to pour alcohol. With or without continued drinking, one of the possible outcomes of this operation is the creation of a "dumping syndrome," in which the patient frequently throws up, very often rejecting the food he requires to nourish himself. After a gastrectomy, one can have a "malabsorption syndrome," with or without dumping, in which the reduced and damaged digestive tract cannot absorb fluids and nourishment adequately. The patient may eat well enough, but he starves because he can't process his food.

Further, no patient should undergo this surgery without being informed that his risk of catching tuberculosis is remarkably enhanced. Many are not told this.

Show me an individual with the familiar "railroad tracks" (operation scars) and tuberculosis and I'll guess present or past severe alcohol problems and be right 80 to 90 percent of the time. Show me a person with alcohol problems and a subtotal gastrectomy, and I'll guess that the person is headed for tuberculosis. The two are related and correlated and mutually causative.

Not all gastritis is caused by alcohol, nor are all ulcers, by any means. But again we usually have ample warning signs, some forgiveness on the part of the body, and plenty of opportunity to save ourselves from horrible pain and troubles.

Any discharge of blood, old and dark or new and bright, has to be checked, whether alcohol-related or not. Belly pain in the presence of heavy drinking may be, or may soon be, accompanied by bleeding.

Peripheral neuropathy, avitaminosis, and cirrhosis tend to be related primarily to heavy chronic drinking of the "late-stage alcoholic" type. Gastritis and ulcers reside somewhat more in heavy social drinkers who are functioning in the community. There are many exceptions, however.

I know of a husband and wife, in their thirties, who are severely alcohol troubled. They can be identified from a social distance if one is alcohol-wise. Strife is apparent; easily sparked and illogical anger spills over onto everybody in the home. There are parties, offers of alcoholic drinks (but nothing else available), and depression, irritability, and fear afterward. At a party, the husband surreptitiously grimaced with pain and tried to hide it. I asked about his pain; he admitted he had it; and I suggested maybe if he cut back on his scotch a bit his belly might not bite him so hard. A week later the word filtered back that he had switched to bourbon, and a week after that I saw him again socially and his belly was still biting him—sudden, intense, sporadic pain. I told my wife on the way home that he looked like a "bleeder" to me and I hoped he'd get to the hospital in time when it happened. Two weeks later he was taken to the emergency room, and he made it for the moment. A bleeder is a person who has an ulcer that produces massive, sudden bleeding that either is not visible because the blood stays in the abdominal cavity, or is evidenced by blood in the stools or rectum. This evidences real danger of emergency surgery and/or death.

I do not know what this man's physician actually told him, but the patient and his wife say they were told that he shouldn't eat so many hot dogs on the run. They made no mention of alcohol. Be that as it may, he's still a potential bleeder and still in alcohol trouble because he's still drinking.

Observers clearly resist perceiving or suspecting an alcohol involvement in people like this—impeccably groomed and dressed, bright, personable, successful, attractive, and well-to-do. This is precisely the kind of situation in which alcohol tends to be overlooked because the drinker isn't a bum.

Another man in his thirties has been packing it away very heavily for years. Suddenly he's exhausted, has no strength, has just quit his relatively sedentary job, and has suddenly turned gray of complexion. I am betting that he's losing blood somewhere. In this case his physician is aware of the alcohol problem because he has told the patient so.

For most problems in alcohol work there is a quick solution—that's the beauty of the field. Each of these serious physical problems has a clear remedy. We'd be in luck if all our physical ills had such ready remedies.

Diabetes

Diabetes mellitus is a disorder of the body's sugar balancing mechanism and is related to drinking and nutrition in that carbohydrate is introduced in unpredictable quantities by alcohol. In diabetics, it is important to keep the carbohydrate intake low *and predictable*. Alcohol troubled people traditionally and quite understandably encounter tremendous difficulty in carrying off the intricate, disciplined, and delicate balancing regimen required of the diabetic, who must juggle carbohydrate and sugar intake, emotional and physical behavior, and medication such as insulin. Since a failure to handle these factors successfully can lead to confusion, irrational and highly anxious behavior, and even coma or death, it is abundantly clear that diabetes and alcohol troubles are a bad mix.

Tuberculosis

Tuberculosis (TB) is commonly understood to have a number of causes, one of which is always that the patient becomes the host of the bacillus or bug. Several factors make the host susceptible to the disease, however. Among these are poverty and the associated physical and emotional stresses. Poor nutrition is paramount among the preparing circumstances and can be related directly to subtotal gastrectomies, as noted earlier. Another circumstance increasing the likelihood of contracting the disease is associating with persons having active tuberculosis in poor sanitary conditions, and one of the best ways to do that is to do your drinking in an inner-city bar.

In a four-year annual survey I conducted in a Veterans Administration tuberculosis ward, I never came up with less that 88 percent alcohol-associated TB, and usually over 90 percent of the population had a significant alcohol problem.

It is generally accepted that there would be *no* TB in the United States were it not for the reservoir of the bacillus in alcohol troubled people. Such individuals, usually malnourished, have difficulty holding still for the six-to eighteen-month treatment required to arrest it. They tend to have severe alcohol problems and can be somewhat emotionally unstable, sometimes hostile, often confused. Started on a course of chemotherapy, in which they may need to take one slow-acting medication or another for months or years, they bolt from the hospital before finishing the treatment. They now carry with them a drug-resistant form, so that the original medication will not help. An example of the same principle occurred when DDT was in wide use—the insects that got a small but not lethal dose of it survived and became DDT-immune.

Alternatively, the TB alcohol patient requires surgery to remove infected tissue and runs from the hospital before the operation can be performed, carrying with him an infectious bug.

Obviously, we cannot attempt to deal with all the physical disorders that tend to afflict the alcohol-prone person, and we will omit reference to many. We will, however, briefly discuss another category of problems directly associated with alcohol usage and also associated with nutritional problems: neurological problems in the central nervous system (brain and spinal column). Neurological disorders present a special class of difficulties because of their direct and specific effect on brain function and thus on thinking, feeling, and perceiving reality.

The word *intoxication* comes from "toxic" or "poison." When a person is intoxicated his brain is temporarily and partially poisoned. If his brain is frequently and heavily poisoned, and if he is also poorly nourished for any reason, and if we consider that the body and the emotions are truly interlocked, we end up with some fairly common neurological problems about which the alcohol worker needs to be aware.

Delirium Tremens

A rough translation of delirium tremens is "shaking delirium," or "shaking temporary insanity." DTs result in a mortality rate of 5 to 25 percent if medically untreated. They usually occur within 72 to 96 hours after cessation of drinking or marked reduction of alcohol intake in persons who have been drinking for at least three weeks and who are also malnourished, whether they've been eating or not. All such persons should be considered to be at very high risk for developing DTs, and steps should be taken to support them physically and emotionally during withdrawal. People in this category should *not* be urged to stop drinking unless they can be followed up and supported during withdrawal. Many severely alcohol-damaged individuals are afraid to stop drinking because they have had "the horrors" before and cannot bear to face them again. It is not widely understood that this is a substantial and valid reason for not wanting to stop.

In addition to the history noted above, people vulnerable to an episode of DTs may be apprehensive and very frightened that something terrible and unnamable may suddenly happen to them. They're quite right. Their eyeballs may be reddened; they may be perspiring. They are shaky, jittery, and overreactive to sounds.

When the episode actually strikes, the individual has hallucinations and delusions that are extremely vivid and realistic. The hallucinations often occur in full color and may take the form of "pink elephants" or a room full of threatening and attacking rats, for example. Like the paranoid person who is being pursued by the FBI or the Martians, the person in DTs is terrified by his false perceptions and beliefs. He may be on the twentieth story of a city hospital and will become exhausted to the point of death by the image of twenty-story-tall people attacking him through the window with knives or octopus tentacles or poison gas. Or he may climb screaming onto his bed to avoid drowning as his room fills rapidly with water gushing from a floor tile. He may leap to his death from the window to escape (not commit suicide, simply escape), or he may suffer a fatal heart attack, or he may become dehydrated.

He will have lucid or rational episodes between hallucinations and should be permitted freedom of movement, perhaps walking about the ward. It is a mistake to put a patient with DTs in mechanical restraints, since it only terrifies him more.

If the admitting people know about DTs they can institute protective measures (replacement of fluids and nourishment, tranquilizing and antiseizure medication, and so on) before the episode hits, measures that will shorten, soften, or prevent the episode. No one, for heaven's sake, needs to die any more.

Physicians, especially in city hospitals, have learned

the value of giving alcohol to DT-vulnerable people if emergency surgery is needed—this alcohol staves off postoperative DTs, during which patients may refracture broken arms that have just been set, rip open sutures, and so forth.

Korsakoff's Psychosis and Wernicke's Disease

Korsakoff's Psychosis and Wernicke's Disease are two related chronic brain problems, clearly of physical origin, associated with the heavy use of alcohol and with poor nutrition. Each is serious and debilitating, and each produces symptoms of "craziness." Korsakoff's is particularly notable for causing striking loss of memory and consequent fabrication of stories to fill the gaps (confabulation), and confusion as to time, place, and person. Wernicke's may be marked by rapid onset of such symptoms as headache, double vision, staggering, and stupor. It is sometimes accompanied by agitation, confusion, and hallucinations, as in DTs. The outcome of either syndrome may be complete recovery, partial recovery, or death. Skid row bums often have these severe organic manifestations of alcohol troubles; they constitute what is known on the street as "wet brain."

Epilepsy or Seizure Disorders

The brain can be regarded as both a generator of electricity and a director and transmitter of electrical messages, similar to a telephone switchboard. The brain wave or electroencephalograph is a machine that records the electrical activity of the brain to produce an electroencephalogram (EEG). Electrodes placed on the scalp and connected by wires to the machine pick up the strength and frequency of brain impulses and transmit them to pens that mark a revolving roll of paper. The marks are interpreted by a neurologist, who can see if the pattern of electric potentials is regular, symmetrical, and of the proper frequency and strength.

If the blood bath in which the brain works has a chemical imbalance (too great or too low a concentration of sugar, hormones, fluid, alcohol, impurities, and so on) the electrical pattern may change. If the brain has suffered mechanical damage, such as a lesion or sore, a blow to the head, or a sudden stoppage of blood as in a stroke, the pattern can also change. Sudden or strong emotion can raise or drop the blood pressure, changing the mechanical and chemical environment; the places in the brain that are affected, as well as the specific ways in which they are affected, can produce different electrical outputs. Thus, a dysfunction in one part of the brain may produce paralysis, while a dysfunction in another part will result in the inability to read, to talk, or to feel in certain areas of the body. The alcohol-involved person is particularly susceptible to complicated neurological difficulties.

Most of us are familiar with epileptic convulsions, or grand mal seizures, in which the subject may fall to the floor and rhythmically contract and relax the big muscle groups. He or she may hold the breath and turn blue from lack of oxygen, bang the head against the floor in the spasms, be unconscious, defecate or urinate, and so forth. These are some of the results of electrical storm activity in the brain—activity that can be brought on by many factors in a vulnerable "machine."

It has long been known that reducing consumption after heavy, prolonged usage of alcohol markedly increases the probability of grand mal convulsions. Since it is desirable to avoid such potentially harmful seizures, heavy drinkers in withdrawal facilities are often given, in their medical "cocktail" (vitamins, tranquilizers, and so on), an anticonvulsant medication to reduce the likelihood of electrical storm activity in the brain.

It is not so widely known, however, that just as there

is an "off" effect, there is also an "on" effect of alcohol in a number of brains vulnerable to electrical storm activity. As the person with the seizure-vulnerable brain *begins* liberal use of alcohol, the brain has to adjust to a new and disrupting chemical bath, and seizure activity may result. Seizure activity may take the form of convulsions, which are easily recognized, but it may instead alter behavior or perception *without* convulsion.

Have you ever seen anybody go absolutely crazy with booze? Or quietly weird and irrational? That may be electrical storm activity.

So there are "off" *and* "on" effects. People being withdrawn from alcohol have a right to be protected, and if you can honestly assure them of protection from their electrical storm fears and bizarre feelings you may be making it possible for them to quit drinking. A person is unlikely to quit if he is feeling frightened, shaky, and weird and knows another drink will take that feeling away, especially if the person trying to convince him doesn't respond in a supporting, understanding, and knowledgeable way.

Crazy and sick he may be, but not that crazy and sick.

Once again, if people have this kind of trouble when they drink they're definitely alcohol troubled, but please don't look for these problems only in severe instances of "alcoholism" or skid row pathology. We have probably all sustained some brain damage somewhere along the line, and under the "right" (or wrong) circumstances our brains are vulnerable to electrical storm activity. You may have been hit on the head by a swing as a kid, or had a high fever, or been knocked out playing football, or been anesthetized to have your baby. You were certainly delivered somehow (high forceps delivery? prolonged labor with not enough oxygen?). Any of these injuries can make you vulnerable.

Alcoholic Blackouts and Temporal Lobe Epilepsy

I have not read or heard of anyone making a connection between alcohol-associated "blackouts" and temporal lobe epilepsy, although I'm sure someone besides me has noticed their remarkable symptomatic similarities. In any event, I propose that they are one and the same thing.

The alcohol-associated "blackout" is misnamed. It should have been called "blank-out." In both this and temporal lobe epilepsy the individual "loses time." He continues to function in a way that is usually not perceived by others as being any different from his usual behavior. Yet he has no ability to recall what occurred in that span of time, which may in fact cover minutes, hours, days, or even weeks.

This is *not* intoxicated "passing out," or falling unconscious to the floor with an overdose of the chemical alcohol, or being poured into bed. The critical issue here is functioning apparently normally while disconnected from recall, and the phenomenon can occur without any alcohol actually in the system. In neurological terms this is called "automatic behavior" or "automatism."

Here are two examples of automatic behavior, one associated with alcohol usage, the other not:

In the first, the individual met a friend on the street and felt a pang of conscience. He regularly went over to his friend's house to play cards with the man and his wife. "Realizing" that he had missed the scheduled evening, he apologized and said he would come over to play the next week. His friend looked at him strangely, hesitated, and said, "Walter, you were with Ida and me last night." He had no recollection, and neither Ida nor her husband had had any inkling that Walter's head was functioning in an unusual fashion. None of the three had been drunk or even drinking.

In the second instance another man, also not drinking that day but a heavy drinker, went to the ocean to do some surf-casting. Two hours later he became conscious of his surroundings; he was sitting in his car faced the wrong way on a one-way street, with a police car blocking his way in front and another behind. The officers had his doors open and had guns trained on him. In the back of his car were several expensive surf rods not owned by him; he was twenty

miles from the rocks from which he had been casting. He
could very well afford to buy, and had no logical need to
steal, the rods in his car trunk.

Neither will ever gain recall regarding those incidents,
since the events were not recorded.

A peculiar rumor in some alcohol circles holds that you
can recall what you did in an "alcoholic blackout" only
when you get drunk again, to reproduce the state in which
you performed the action. Nonsense. I heard that one again
recently in a lecture in which the speaker had no apparent
awareness that she had just (correctly) stated that the
individual is not necessarily intoxicated during the blackout.
Oh, well.

You may have run across one of those lists that suggests that if you're having "blackouts" you're an alcoholic.
Maybe, although a fair number of people have temporal lobe
episodes not related to alcohol. You do have alcohol troubles
if your lost time is associated with the use of alcohol; recall
that alcohol can have both an "on" effect and an "off" effect
with regard to triggering electrical storms.

It is more useful to note that your brain may be vulnerable to electrical storm activity under certain circumstances, and that alcohol intake is traditionally one of those
circumstances. Even a small amount of alcohol (the "on"
situation) may trigger the brain into electrical storms. If
your brain is not vulnerable to seizure activity unless you
drink a fair amount and suffer nutritional deficit and you
start to get in that condition, then you are in my view damaging your brain in the temporal lobe area and are having
symptoms of temporal lobe epilepsy, which you are free to
call blackouts if you wish.

I commend to the serious reader in this area the book
Ictal and Sub-Ictal Neuroses by A. D. Jonas, published by
Charles Thomas. It may be hard reading for the nonprofessional, but it's short and excellent. I believe it to be essential
reading for any health or mental health helper.

As Jonas points out, another possible expression of

seizure activity is the sensation of weirdness or bizarre ideas and feelings. I well recall a patient referred to me in my younger days by a clever neurologist as a demonstration. "What do you think is his diagnosis?" he asked. I knew the patient had a drinking problem of serious proportions, that he was unfortunate enough to work in a brewery with the policy of "All you can drink as you work," that he was subject to lost-time episodes, and that he displayed bizarre behavior. I talked to him and discovered that he was only mildly puzzled that he could occasionally see the back of his own head, that it was shaped like the prow of a ship, and that it was composed of black, shiny glass. That was enough for me. "Schizophrenic," said I. I watched the "schizophrenia" clear with rest, no alcohol, good food, therapeutic vitamins, and no tranquilizers or psychotherapy. It was, of course, temporal lobe confusion.

A special note to mental health professionals: Occasionally in your clinical practice you run into "lost-time" cases, as I have. You have been trained to view these aberrations as either "amnesia," a "fugue state," or a "dissociative reaction." Please consider the possibility of a temporal lobe problem, and, having done that, check out the alcohol to see if you are in fact dealing with the special form of temporal lobe epilepsy which can be called an alcohol and nutritional deficit "blackout." If your experience is at all like mine you will never again see a functional, or non-organic, dissociative reaction. Try it, at least. And if you always probe the "lost-time" possibility you will locate a surprising number of cases, even in little kids with no alcohol problem.

I will skip the beri-beri heart disease, the savagely painful pancreatitis in which the pancreas may actually digest itself and the stomach wall, the repeated pneumonias, and many other alcohol-associated disorders.

I refer only in passing to the huge number of accidents that are associated with alcohol misuse. A magic figure of 50 percent or thereabouts keeps recurring in alcohol work.

About 50 percent of fatal auto accidents are associated with intoxication-level blood alcohol, as are drownings. I don't know the figures on broken bones, lacerated heads, and falls from ladders, but I rather doubt whether we collect statistics on such everyday accidents.

People keep telling me that the "alcoholic," by which they sometimes mean "the intoxicant" and sometimes the "late-stage, chronic alcoholic" (but almost never the minimally or moderately affected person), has a lifespan shortened by an average of ten to twelve years. Maybe so. I don't think we can yet put a number on it, but I can completely agree that the life of a heavy drinker is significantly shortened. Even people who spend time around ATPs have shorter lives, since a high proportion of homicides occur under the influence. And suicides.

The important point is that if you look at physical damage and the presence of alcohol, you will be able to identify many ATPs before you would otherwise. Then, instead of trumpeting the word "alcoholic," try to ease or at least deal with the trouble.

I have tried to direct the reader's attention, whenever possible, toward true preventive efforts and/or intervention techniques that can be used earlier in the development of the trouble than is now generally the case.

It can be quite helpful in this regard to utilize the "three-legged stool" concept; if two conditions exist that have a high correlation with the abuse of alcohol, assume that there will be a third leg to the stool—alcohol troubles. The concept works most clearly with physical problems, but it can be applied to elements from the social, financial, and emotional areas of our definition as well.

Suppose an individual comes to a hospital emergency room with (1) a broken bone and (2) a history of repeated pneumonia. It is reasonable to suppose that the question of (3) alcohol trouble should be examined.

Suppose a person (1) is depressed and (2) has a hemigastrectomy scar, having undergone an operation for "intractable" stomach ulcers. Since the first two conditions occur very frequently in the presence of (3) alcohol troubles, it is reasonable to assume, or to check out, that possibility.

Tuberculosis and malnutrition also could be two legs. So could diabetes that is hard to control and epilepsy. Repeated job changes and relationship difficulties in the family could also qualify as two legs of the stool, and so forth.

A discussion of physical components of alcohol troubles is an appropriate place for a word about the popular disease concept of alcoholism. I am aware that the American Medical Association officially declared alcoholism a disease in 1956, even though many physicians and hospitals still refuse to label or treat it.

I am aware also that AA calls alcoholism a disease (among other things), that the National Council on Alcoholism does, and that the National Institute for Alcohol Abuse and Alcoholism also does.

There have been pragmatic, practical reasons for calling alcoholism an illness or disease, and probably the current high level of funding and the decriminalization laws flowed from this trend.

I have no wish to stir up controversy in this regard (although I am quite willing and even eager to do so in other regards), and I am acutely aware that I will anger many people with my position. Yet I believe the disease notion to be inaccurate. I believe alcohol troubles are the outcome of *learning* a way to cope with one's anxiety by means of a chemical. And mine is a point of view shared by many, and I believe a growing number of people.

These things tend to go in popular, faddist cycles, and I believe someday we will drop the disease concept simply because it is not correct and leads us into philosophical, scientific, and treatment error.

I do not say, as some antidisease adherents do, that to let the disease concept stand is to let the "alcoholic" excuse his "immoral" and "willful" behavior, for I do not believe that those terms should even enter into a reasoned discussion of the difficulties. We do know for sure that a lot of people in trouble with alcohol have learned to get in trouble and can also learn, sometimes quite quickly, to get out of it.

If people drink in certain ways with certain kinds of bodies, personalities, and circumstances, then they can *develop* a disease process, or several processes. Drinking can readily *lead* to disease, but the act or habit of drinking does not itself constitute a disease.

This section has dealt with some of the many physical problems that are caused, at least in part, by alcohol ingestion. I insist that alcohol *leads to* a multiplicity of diseases, and that after these diseases or damages take hold one can be dealing with a sick, ill, or diseased organism.

But damaging drinking is not a disease. It's a series of *acts*, *learned* to serve a maladaptive purpose, and quite subject to a process of relearning.

Emotional Components

I have developed elsewhere the general proposition that the very use of alcohol, whether in a troubling way or not, is based on its ability to alter our feelings and perceptions. It is a consciousness-altering chemical that has all the properties of a drug, and an addicting one at that.

To state, as I have, that man in the generic sense uses alcohol to reduce immediate feelings of tension (usually anxiety and depression) by learning to take advantage of its mind-and-feeling-bending properties is different from discussing the emotional component of the definition of alcohol troubles. To describe why a person drinks I have postulated a causative, etiological relationship between the existence of the discomfort or pain of anxiety and the use of alcohol.

Now, however, we need to examine behavior to determine whether alcohol usage lowers the quality of life in the emotional area. Should we find such emotional problems we will have developed a means by which we can identify alcohol damage in a critical life area and can then be sure that alcohol troubles are present. Having accomplished this identification we can then proceed in individual and program situations in a clear-thinking, helpful fashion.

We will also have clarified for ourselves and for the impaired person that there is a physical involvement from which we can expect certain eventual consequences, since, as noted before, it is not possible to have emotions without physical reaction.

Technically, emotion means the area of feelings. In practice, it is necessary to include in emotion the thinking, or cognitive, process, since there is a remarkably close interaction between the two. Most people have experienced a definite reluctance to turn off the last light after the conclusion of a vampire show on TV. Your emotions seem to overcome your cognitive processes. Common sense suggests that the house is just as safe as it was before the TV movie, but on the other hand you're afraid and begin to imagine strange things and sounds. Even familiar shadows look like lurking creatures.

I remember visiting a young farmer friend in Maine. He and his wife had just purchased a large tract of land and were struggling desperately to hold on until they could get a couple of cash crops in. He went deer hunting with his dog, and getting the deer was important in terms of eating. He saw a flash of white in the brush, double-checked, saw his "deer," and killed it. It proved to be his dog, a fluffy brown creature with a white underside to its tail. My friend couldn't believe what he had done. He had been hunting enough not to shoot at sounds, and he had actually "seen" a buck deer when he was looking at his familiar dog, which was the size of a springer spaniel.

Emotion alters perception (what we see, hear, feel) and cognition (what we think).

I have noted earlier that man drinks in the face of, and

to reduce, anxiety and its close cousin, depression, and that over the long haul this mode of coping with these feelings is counterproductive simply on a chemical basis.

Alcoholics Anonymous people often talk about "stinkin' thinkin'," which is an excellent phrase for describing the ATP's impaired judgment. He overreacts or underreacts, makes important decisions when irritable or confused or feeling picked on. He may even tell you, while in this state, that he's now so in control of his drinking that he tests himself by eating his lunch in a bar. Bars are alcohol outlets, and one eats lunch in a restaurant or out in the sun with a brown paper bag. The guy who buys milk in a bar is doing a bit of stinkin' thinkin', and we can safely state that he's in trouble with booze even though he's not drinking it right at the moment.

Attempts are constantly being made to characterize ATPs as having a standard alcohol-type personality, even though that effort is repeatedly unfruitful. Some call ATPs unreliable, but many severely alcohol-impaired people are highly reliable. They are said by some to have orally dependent character disorders, but that doesn't hold up on inspection either. They are said in some circles to be liars, on the grounds that they have lied to themselves and can easily do so to others, and anyway that's what "alcoholics" are. I find many nonliars in the alcohol troubled category, although it is clearly wisest to be careful not to accept every statement as gospel. Engaging in deception or self-deception is not so clearly an alcohol-associated characteristic that it helps us in any practical way to separate those who are in drinking trouble from those who aren't.

I once attended a lecture on "alcoholism" in which the speaker contended that "the name of the game is denial." Sure. Big help. Show me the nondrinking executive who comes home from work and eagerly volunteers to his wife, "I lost that big contract today because I was stupid. I added the figures wrong, I didn't do my homework, and I got into a foolish argument about civil rights with Mr. Big."

Within two days of the loss of the contract the whole thing is transmuted in Charlie's eyes so that he can quite genuinely (because by now he honestly believes it) blame a secretary, a vice-president, or the home office and its rigid bureaucratic policies. That, too, is denial.

Several years ago I played tennis about ten times with a nondrinking psychologist and beat him relatively handily each time. He had a reason for each loss. He had a cold or was overtrained or the balls were too old or too new or too nonstandard or the wind was too strong or the net was too high or the court not regulation size. He *still* thinks he can beat me, because his denial system will not tolerate the notion that a slob can beat an athlete like him.

The characterization of the ATP that comes closest for me is that you don't have to scratch very deeply through the veneer to find an angry, hostile person. I believe this often is quite true, but I realize that it is often true also of people who do not have alcohol troubles.

On the other hand, there are theoretical reasons for believing that anger underlies alcohol troubles: Depression typically occurs in the face of loss or of anger so privately handled that it gets turned back on the self. The loss can be past, present, or future, and it can be the loss of youth or health or job or love or self-esteem. People even get angry (and depressed, which is another expression of exactly the same thing) in an unconscious way at the death of a loved one, thus the half-joking expression, "He loved me, but he died." Emotionally, they feel that if he really loved me he would have done me the courtesy of hanging around.

Many, many people—an astounding number—simply cannot bring themselves to express anger at other people, or even to *think* it. It is too frightening and uncomfortable, for a number of reasons we can't go into here. For such people it is literally unthinkable to tell another person directly he doesn't like to be kept waiting, or to be put down, or to have his person or self-esteem damaged. These are the ones who, if the dentist hurts them unnecessarily, never say, "Do that an easier way for me next time, even if it takes you an extra three minutes." Instead they say, "Oh, that's OK," when it isn't OK.

Such people are especially subject to depression, because the anger *does go somewhere*. It doesn't evaporate. It gets turned inward. It is healthier to make the admittedly immature but at least openly annoyed comment, "Look what you made me do," than not to permit annoyance to show.

Alcohol-damaged people are fairly famous for feeling spurts of remorse and guilt. The feelings may not last long enough to make them quit drinking, but if one can think of it as a form of anger, it can be used helpfully. Anger is a better energizer than its offshoot, depression, so to the extent that one can uncover and identify anger one can use it. It's easier to steer a moving automobile than to get one with a sputtering engine moving, which is simply another way of saying that if alcohol-oriented people are indeed fairly angry (as well as fairly depressed) that fact is useful in efforts to be of help, provided the helper can make use of the anger instead of feeling clobbered by it.

It is extremely important to investigate the alcohol situation in all people who come to your mental health clinic, or hospital, or private practice. Much that appears under traditional classifications to be grist for the mental health mill is, in fact, amenable to positive alteration only after the alcohol issue is successfully addressed. This clearly holds true for anxiety reactions and depressions. It is also true for some of the apparent schizophrenias (not all of them, but enough to make it essential to check out the alcohol possibility). Any disorder characterized by irrationality and illogic, unstable affect or emotion, overreaction, irritability, and marital and family breakdown are suspect for alcohol.

Mental health patients (people with emotional problems) are generated in great numbers by alcohol usage. "Mental health" disorders, be they neuroses, psychotic adjustments, vocational difficulties, or whatever, can be and are surprisingly often the direct consequence of drinking. One gets nowhere by not dealing with the essential cause.

It would probably make sense to insert in the *Diagnostic and Statistical Manual* such diagnostic statements as "Depressive Reaction, alcohol-associated," or "Anxiety Reaction, alcohol-associated," or "Transient Situational Adjustment Reaction, alcohol-associated."

No mental disorder improves with alcohol; most drinking patients have increased symptoms, often directly attributable to the drug and disappearing with its removal. If you're a professional, try to put these concepts to work. I guarantee that you'll find them helpful, and so will your clients.

In summary, if an individual is having trouble associated with the use of alcohol in *any one* of four important life areas—social, financial, physical, or emotional—that person is impaired, damaged, or troubled by alcohol.

It may not do to call him or her an "alcoholic"; try the ATP concept.

It *will not* do to require him or her to be massively damaged, or damaged in all the areas, as a condition of definition (see also Chapter 5 on categories of alcohol troubles).

Alcohol problems tend to camouflage or mask themselves as social, financial, physical, and emotional problems. It is necessary to look behind the screen.

5
Categories or Degrees of Alcohol Troubles

The apple never falls very far from the tree.

He didn't suck that out of his thumb.
Kentucky Folk Sayings,
Courtesy W. C. Redmon

A massive body of literature, myth, and concern is directed toward late, or late middle, stages of alcoholism. It is accurate to say that most of our communications about the problem really focus on the already *severe* case. It is appropriate that we should be deeply and gravely concerned about this aspect of the issues for this is where people die or become desperately damaged. Many people who read this book in the hope of obtaining some clarification of alcohol problems may be entrapped in the severe stages, either in themselves or in members of their families. This entrapment occurs because we are uninformed and unattuned to early intervention.

There is a crying need, however, for increased sensitivity on the part of those who work in the alcohol area and those who suffer from alcohol problems. It has been said, probably with considerable validity, that we could muster all our present treatment facilities, multiply them by ten, and still not reduce the problem significantly. Since most of our treatment and thinking is directed toward severe "alcoholism," we are having little impact. By using this antiquated system, we elect *not* to treat most of our citizens who have alcohol problems. We fail to engage them in AA or any other treatment system. We generate more new "alcoholics" each year than we "cure" or "arrest," whatever your preference regarding the terms. We would be inundated even worse than we are with waves of alcohol-damaged persons were it not for the ecologically sound but humanistically and economically unhappy tendency of the alcohol-involved individual to die early from a multitude of unpleasantries detailed elsewhere in this book.

If larger segments of the population, particularly young persons who still have greater options of flexibility, were to become *informed and alerted* to the issues, we could make real progress. If we continue to invest the bulk of our money, human resources, research, and philosophies into "late-stage" people, we will continue to be grossly ineffective in terms of the total problem. Addictive processes are treated better and more quickly when undertaken early.

We must find ways to intervene earlier, certainly without sacrificing those already in trouble if possible, but in any event in ways that hold real promise of *reducing the total problem*.

As a groundwork, let's investigate the general notion of stages, categories, or *degrees* of alcohol troubles in the hope that by so doing we may refocus attention, directions, and goals in more realistic ways.

Each of the categories about to be discussed is an approximation. Certainly one does not have to fill each condition or criterion within a category to fall into that category. And, as we deal with the categories, recall that all degrees of alcohol involvement are cast against a background of the definition given earlier—if an individual continues to drink even though the quality of his or her life declines in the social, financial, physical, *or* emotional area, he or she *has a problem* with alcohol.

The purposes of this chapter are essentially:

1. To emphasize that current efforts to deal with alcohol problems are almost always based on conceptualizations of late, advanced, severe instances of alcohol involvement and that this focus is in the long run ineffectual.

2. To point out that we will make more progress if we redefine our terms. We retain the notion of alcoholism in progressive stages—early, middle, and late. I propose that we begin to think instead of a different system of categorization—severe, moderate, and minimal. I will also propose and discuss a fourth category—high risk.

3. To deal with stumbling blocks, inaccuracies, and inefficiencies caused by our present untenable tendency to believe that alcohol disorders always follow a chronological progression—from early to middle to late stages.

Severe Category—Late Stage or Advanced

Present terminology—late, middle, early stages—implies that there is a definite chronological, or time, relationship among the stages of alcohol troubles. It is sometimes true that severe problems occur after a period of time, but it would perhaps be more accurate to label the condition "very serious," or "tremendously damaged" rather than "late stage." I prefer "severe."

Later in this chapter I will attempt to clarify some problems inherent in using terms that imply progression as a function of passage of time. For the moment, we can say that part of the problem is that many people drink heavily for years before they show loss of quality in their lives. Sometimes they never demonstrate a loss of quality, but instead foul up our system by dying of natural causes after having consumed three quarts of wine or a fifth of scotch a day for six or seven decades.

Others are destroyed in a year or two, and many fall somewhere in between.

Generally, however (and I am reluctant to put this notion on paper for fear someone will exclude himself inappropriately), severe alcohol damage occurs after five to fifteen years of reasonably heavy imbibing. Severe cases may well suffer serious loss of quality in all four areas in the definition. In any case, they show *serious* problems in at least one area.

When viewing a severe case, only a blind person would fail to note the seriousness of the condition; it is amazing how many spouses, clergymen, employers, psychologists, and physicians have limited vision.

I know a man who was confined to a wheelchair by paralysis from the waist down, who was unable to obtain alcohol unless his wife bought it, who had been hospitalized *specifically* for malnutrition and alcohol withdrawal at least three times, who had suffered DTs on at least two of those occasions, and whose wife continued to buy him his alcohol. "He gets grouchy if I don't get it," was her response. I don't know whether she has gotten the message yet. My latest understanding was that he wasn't drinking—I think that is because *he* got the message—but if he began insisting again, the dutiful wife probably would start bringing liquor home again.

Generally, persons with severe cases have built up tolerance, gradually requiring increasing amounts of alcohol to achieve a given effect. Usually, also, they have reached the level at which their tolerance is beginning to "break"— that is, they "can't drink the way I used to." Often but not always, they could put away prodigious amounts of booze when at the peak of their tolerance, and the peak may have lasted several years. Now, one drink, or half what they used to drink, "knocks me on my ass," or causes their abused stomachs to bleed, or kicks off an episode of truly crazy behavior, violent hostility, or another reaction.

Generally, severe cases do not withdraw comfortably,

although here again there are exceptions—most notably the person who goes the route of weekend or binge drinking. Plenty of people drink in that fashion without ever becoming physiologically addicted or suffering withdrawal pains, although they may be systematically destroying themselves and their families by their drinking pattern.

Again the useful simplicity of our definition becomes evident—one does not need to drink every day, or be addicted, or suffer in withdrawal in order to be in alcohol trouble, even severe trouble. One needs only to be having serious problems from drinking.

These facts seem to be consistent with the observation that helpers repeatedly encounter even "late stage" people who simply quit when informed of what they themselves had not yet seen—a serious tearing of the fabric of their lives through the misuse of alcohol. The odds that a person will quit this way are of course vastly reduced in severe instances.

The argument that anyone who gets out of alcohol trouble quickly "wasn't really an alcoholic" reveals that the speaker lacks experience with some varieties of alcohol-involved people. That such incidents do occur, probably mostly in hospital settings and physicians' offices, is, in fact, an impressive argument for instituting alcohol education programs in places where the knowledge and sensitization such programs provide can be translated into lives, or dollars, or pain saved. If the old-time hard-liners would accept this truth they would spread the word that they in fact want to spread—even "late-stage" alcoholics can be helped, or can learn to help themselves.

Another story illustrates another aspect of alcohol involvement—the fact that many persons who are in the grip of "late stage" problems continue to function in responsible jobs, often for years. No attempt will be made to protect the innocent—the subject of my concern is not likely to read this anyway, and if he does, he will probably continue to deny what he would see in others. And, since he used to be a friend of mine, and I continue to value him as a human being, and because he used to grapple with issues of humanitarian and nonviolent concerns, maybe—just maybe—he will read this and be helped to get help.

He is a physician of Irish-American extraction whose belief in his childhood religion, Roman Catholicism, is now shattered. He sired several children while still adhering to the church's stand on birth control. His mother, toward whom he held very strong feelings of love and respect, as well as secret feelings of anger, grew old and died. All this was occurring as he grew more and more troubled about our involvement in the Vietnam war and about his inability to save all (or even enough) of the patients who came onto his ward in a public medical hospital. The loss of his patients was not his fault, although he had indeed permitted the character of his ward to drift toward the chronic treatment of chronic diseases; that in turn flowed from his basically very decent desire to help those to whom no one else would give much time.

His wife, also of Irish-American background, came on stronger and stronger as he faced a set of changing life circumstances, and another woman came into the picture—superficially warmer and more giving than the wife. Her appearance on the scene further shattered his weakened religious resolve.

At this time, he received on his ward a patient about twenty years old who was to die, over a two-year period, of Hodgkin's disease, despite heroic efforts and involvement on the part of the physician. In many ways the patient was mature beyond his years, but in his anger at having to die so young, he began to strike out at those who were to live longer than he, and who did not yet have to face the psychic and physical pain of dying. Unfortunately, the patient had a very clever unconscious mind, and it cast about for ways to destroy his physician—the man who was trying so hard to save him, but who had been forced by his own beliefs and basic honesty to reveal the almost hopeless prognosis.

The patient, who happened to be lean and sandy-haired, began to read theological texts. He grew a beard and began to speak like an Old Testament prophet. And suddenly he was transformed into a pained, mystical, bearded figure almost great enough to forgive his physician—the man who was crucifying him. Even I, involved peripherally in the case and not of a religious turn of mind, would occasionally feel a chill in the patient's presence—he had become Jesus Christ. He looked like the pictures of Christ. He was in undeniable pain. He spouted powerful theological and emotional jargon. His eyes burned. He did not follow his physician's orders and thus threw away whatever slim chance he had. And, like Christ, he required something—guilt and a change of values—of those who would outlive him.

The physician had been a very heavy drinker for a number of years. His intake increased. He developed spider angiomas (the little spider-shaped burst blood vessels at the surface of the skin, which can be indicative of deep alcohol involvement). His judgment began to slide, and he changed from a friendly, if shy, decent person into a cantankerous, easily triggered reservoir of anger and explosive verbal hostility. He began to make medical errors. One night, while driving with his wife, he completely lost his sense of direction at an interchange on a major, high-speed turnpike, and drove onto it *against oncoming traffic!*

He could not hear any discussion of alcohol, whether presented by his wife, by me, or by medical colleagues.

It is now several years later. He continues to practice medicine, presumably using poorer and poorer judgment but still energetically denying the problem. He no longer lives with his wife and children, nor do they benefit much from his continued excellent income, because he now supports another home. His wife is working, but their once-lovely house suffers from obvious neglect.

He is a late-stage, or advanced stage, or severe ATP. Despite his liver damage, he has remained in the severe category for at least four years. He could be dead or institutionalized tomorrow, or he could continue for four or five more years. The road back becomes more difficult as time goes by—for the sake of his patients he should be dismissed, but if he were, his way back would be more difficult. Yet he should either deliver what he is hired for or face the music—and facing the music might well be what he needs.

Moderate Category

There can be no clear line of demarcation between moderate and severe alcohol involvement. The same criteria are used—financial, social, physical, or emotional problems —but probably in the last analysis the observer's informed sense of values is the best yardstick. My own beliefs and experiences suggest that somewhere along the line the physical area becomes exceedingly important. Thus, if an individual has an episode of DTs or has liver damage, I regard him as severe. Imminent life risk always connotes advanced involvement to me, whether it be from a diabetes/alcohol interaction or a pattern of automobile accidents.

Failure to advance on the job due to alcohol-associated poor judgment I would put in the moderate category; likewise beginning but chronic physical symptomatology. A couple of job losses due to alcohol generally indicate moderate involvement, whereas virtual or imminent loss of a *career* evidences a severe case. Increased tolerance to alcohol effects is seen in the moderate category, whereas a break in tolerance is severe.

Family and marital problems that threaten long-term adjustment are severe (wife about to leave, children failing in school or in their development of life-long trust patterns), whereas marital and family frictions that cause temporary unhappiness or reversible problems in kids denote moderate damage.

Any hospitalization is severe. Many physicians' warnings, if delivered in an outpatient or office setting, occur in instances of moderate involvement (although depending on other circumstances they could be placed in the minimal or severe pigeonholes). A factor here, of course, is the degree to which the physician knows his subject. Some, highly informed and sensitized, are able to counsel high-risk persons who have no current problem, whereas other physicians commit gastrectomies on people without awareness that they are performing major surgery on a severe alcohol-associated disorder.

People can be, paradoxically, in the severe category for years (always in great jeopardy) and others may be in the moderate category only briefly—another indication that categories or degrees should be based on erosion of quality of life, not on time taken to reach a certain state.

As mentioned before, we almost always, and repeatedly, face emotional depression in alcohol work. Yet how do we measure the seriousness of the depression when it is so often masked and camouflaged as something else? Striking, undisguised sadness, tears, guilt, "blues," or suicidal behavior are quickly identifiable as depression, but how many of us zero in on the manifold other faces of depression?

An almost infallible sign is the specific sleep disorder in which the sufferer seems to fall asleep fairly well but wakes in the wee hours of the morning, cannot "turn off" his thoughts, and lies awake until 5:30 or 6:00 or sleeps during the day.

Difficulty in making decisions is also an often-ignored but useful index to depression. In severe cases people sometimes *cannot* decide which shoe to put on first in the morning, or whether to wash the dishes or make the beds, and therefore stay in bed.

Loss of energy is a good indicator of depression.

Often, moderate to severe depression is expressed in somatic complaints, including headache, back problems, muscle spasms, loss or increase in appetite (and thus weight), digestive problems, and the like.

A reasonably sophisticated judgment as to severity of depression is necessary in order to assign a case to the moderate or severe category of alcohol involvement.

The same is true in judging the quality of cognitive, or thinking, activities. Clinical decisions are of necessity subjective in nature—the helper has to determine the seriousness of the individual's loss of ability to arrive at rational conclusions. Sometimes irrationality is first perceived in moderately foolish pronouncements that seem to be embedded in the drinker's overemotional (usually angry or "ego-trip") behavior.

In an alcohol program to which I was a consultant, an alcohol troubled physician—very bright, verbal, and supposedly nondrinking—attacked a nonalcoholic staff member and arranged that this competent person not perform first-contact interviews. The rationale was incompetent and the argument was much too vociferous and ego-involved. The staff uncritically accepted the ATP's argument, probably as much to avoid a confrontation as anything, and a month or two later were forced by circumstances to conclude that he had been drinking and popping pills for several months.

The individual in question is late stage, advanced, or, in the system used here, severe.

Another means for winnowing out moderate from severe cases is based on the level of self-confidence. Very often the severely damaged individual has made so many bad judgments that he begins to doubt himself, or more accurately, his own relationship to reality; the moderate person is getting there, but he may retain his confidence in his own abilities.

The severe person, even if he is "arrested" or sober for a considerable period of time, is likely to reveal his loss of self-belief in one or both of two ways:

1. He may become dependent on others for decision-making, particularly when the decisions have important implications. He abdicates the throne of self-direction,

an act that in itself does not enhance his self-esteem. If in a position of authority, he may wiggle and squirm to make it appear that he is deciding, but careful scrutiny will reveal that he is not.

2. He may indulge in what psychologists call "reaction formation"—in an effort to deny what is happening to him, in this case loss of self-confidence, he acts supremely self-confident, even though he may be relying on others.

The person who has lost self-confidence reveals himself to the tuned-in observer. The supposedly self-confident person of this kind is threatened by adequate behavior on the part of others. He may, for example, bluff a decision that turns out to be a poor one. If he was depending on the judgment of others, he will blame them. If he makes an incorrect judgment in opposition to suggestions from others, and their judgment is vindicated, he will be so uncomfortable at the demonstration of the gap between himself and them that he will try to punish or avoid them.

He suffers from alcohol problems of the severe type.

Again, judging a person to be in one or another of the categories places a demand on the personal judgment of the categorizer. Generally, thinking of the amount of damage in each of the four areas of our definition will help a lot. And remember, just as you need loss of quality in *only one* of the four areas to diagnose an alcohol problem, so do you need severe or serious damage in *only one* of the four areas to judge that the individual has a severe degree of involvement. Severely alcohol troubled persons very often (but not always) fall into most or all of the four areas.

The wife of an ambitious young executive who drinks in such a way that she overreacts to a social situation at a company party and runs out of the boss's house and down the icy street in ten-degree weather without shoes or outer clothing is close to being severe. She runs an excellent risk of doing serious damage to the fiscal, the social and family, the emotional, and the physical parts of her life.

Yet, even if she ends up being hospitalized for emotional disturbance for a few days, she may be in no more difficulty than the wife of a working man who manages somehow to do her housework, satisfy her husband, and not get sick—yet consumes a fifth of scotch a day at six dollars a bottle. The second woman, remarkably, may be damaging only the family finances at the moment, yet she is in as much trouble as the first woman; both suffer from a severe degree of alcohol involvement.

Minimal Category

The ideas in this section sometimes generate a good deal of criticism from the "hard-liners," who say that there is no such thing as a "little bit of alcoholism"—any more than one can be a little bit pregnant. Still, a lot of people really and truly have troubles with alcohol, but not big troubles or even medium troubles.

Sometimes people with little booze problems progress rather steadily toward bigger problems. But sometimes they don't.

How about the guy who stops at the local pub every Friday night with his $120 paycheck, blows twenty dollars of it and four hours in cards, good masculine fellowship, and so on, and arrives home at about 10 or 11 o'clock to a disgruntled, unhappy wife?

No big deal. No divorce, no sickness, no real craziness. A lot of guys do it, right? It's only 17 percent of his take-home pay.

He's the same guy who goes hunting with the same boys with cases of beer. They live like pigs for four days, are mellow for most of it, and have a great time. Usually one of the five gets his deer and they only rarely blow a kid off his bicycle or send a fellow hunter prematurely to the Happy Hunting Ground.

Those are problems in the quality of living. They aren't big ones, though. And if someone argues that anyone who lives this way will progress to moderate or severe degrees of problems with booze, I can point out ten of them who haven't and probably won't.

If, on the other hand, someone insists that this is the pool from which tremendous numbers of moderate and severe alcohol problems develop, I would most heartily agree.

As you can see, many paradoxes, inconsistencies, and distortions enter into the ways in which we consider alcohol issues.

We have come, then, to another paradox, to wit—

Those who contend that there's no such thing as a minimal degree of alcoholism, who consider such a phrase to be a contradiction in terms, necessarily tend to think of alcoholism as being present only when severe, or late-stage. You have to be very sick to have one of these helpers be willing to help you. To them, the only alcoholic worthy of the name is a *late stage* alcoholic. And he or she has to "hurt enough" to want help.

If a psychologist, psychiatrist, physician, or other professional fails to note the presence of minimal alcohol problems, he or she has made a grievous error of omission. Such accusations are regularly made, and quite properly in many cases, but *everyone* working in the field, "professional" or not, must learn that early identification and intervention are important.

Suppose, for example, that an unknown number of persons come into possession of this book in order to deal better with an alcohol problem in someone else in the family. Suppose further that they become aware that persons in the alcohol-damaged person's family are at higher risk for the development of alcohol problems than are others. Then it becomes important to note that there are *different degrees* of severity, that people can do something useful about drinking patterns *before addiction or destruction occurs,* and that they can sort out the issues more easily by referring to our four-part definition.

It is foolish to beg society to attend to alcohol problems

more energetically and helpfully than it does and then to deny that people can be helped sooner and better than they have in the past.

I like to work with people who have alcohol problems of all degrees of severity, although I am convinced that we must learn to attend better to the developing problems much earlier than we have done so far. Those who wish to devote most of their energies to the severest problems are and should be free to do so, but we all need to make common cause. We have enough problems from outside our ranks.

For the past several years I have taught an undergraduate course called "Psychological and Social Aspects of Alcoholism." It has become a custom to ask the students at the first class meeting to write anonymously why they selected the course and what they wish to get out of it. A few write simply, "An *A*" or "Three Credits."

That's straightforward enough.

But about half want to go into social work or nursing or some other field in which a knowledge of the subject would be useful.

The other half takes the course for personal reasons. "Wonder if I have a problem." "My father died of it last year." "I want to find out how to get help for my mother."

Each year I try to get the prerequisites for the course changed in the university catalog. They now read:
1. Psychology *X* [an introductory psych course having absolutely *nothing* to do with mine].
2. Junior or Senior standing (I have been convinced for some time that freshmen and sophomores and their alcohol-involved families would benefit most from early information).
3. Permission of the Instructor.

Personally, my only prerequisite is that the students have a high school diploma, and that isn't truly necessary either. Each year I am unsuccessful in eliminating the requirements, but I suppose I will make it eventually.

Faced with that kind of reasoning from outside our ranks, we need to pull together better.

High-Risk Category

In addition to intervening early in existing problems, we must all become involved in actual prevention. We must apply the things we know about what makes people especially vulnerable to alcohol difficulties.

Obviously, large numbers of people develop alcohol problems without anyone suspecting that they are at risk. Part of the explanation is certainly our general abysmal ignorance as a society, yet we are now in a position to reduce that ignorance. We know, in fact, that individuals with certain kinds of histories and value systems are particularly vulnerable. Clearly, we do not know all there is to know, or perhaps even half of what we will someday know. That is not the same as saying that we know nothing useful.

Medicine in several areas has developed systematic structures of knowledge by means of which predictions of risk can be made. We are aware, for example, that the risk of heart disease and sudden coronary attacks is significantly increased in people who are: (1) male, (2) over forty, (3) overweight; (4) heavy users of nicotine, (5) anxious, striving, ambitious overworkers and overworriers, (6) non-exercisers or sporadic exercisers, and (7) from families with a history of coronary disease. The likelihood that a person will someday have a heart attack increases cumulatively with the number of items in the list that apply to him. Of course, there are "false positives"—people who have all these signs but who never develop bad hearts. There are also "false negatives"—individuals who fit none of the criteria but nevertheless sustain serious heart damage. Nobody, then, says that a lean, exercising, calm, vocationally satisfied, nonsmoking woman of thirty cannot have a heart attack. But on an overall statistical table of probabilities—the percentage likelihood—her chances are far lower than the high-risk male just described.

If one can develop in helpers an awareness of high-risk potentials, then some of the conditions ordinarily associated with heart attack can be altered *before* the attack occurs, thus lessening its likelihood. This, of course, is true prevention.

As mentioned before, many persons who are interested in alcohol-associated problems have fallen into the habit of accepting only severe alcohol troubles as a true manifestation of the problems. A major purpose of this book is to try to alert helpers to the existence of less severe (minimal and moderate) degrees of categories of the disorder and thereby to help them become more willing and able to intervene earlier and more effectively. Clearly, such an outlook can enable us to see ourselves (as helpers), the problem, and its reduction in far more optimistic terms. "Cures" or "arrests," whichever you like best philosophically, should be counted as just that even when they occur simply and quickly as a result of an informed person telling the alcohol-involved individual what he is doing. There is no advantage to insisting that alcoholism or alcohol troubles are more difficult to repair than they actually are.

So the distinction between the minimal, moderate, and severe degrees has been made here (1) to encourage helpers and ATPs alike to begin work quickly and appropriately, (2) to increase the success rate, and (3) to tell everybody that we have already increased it and can do better. In turn we can reduce stigma, reduce denial of the problem in sufferers and their families, and increase optimism markedly and honestly. There are manifold advantages to doing this.

But all this would be, in fact, merely early, or earlier, identification of and intervention in *an already existing problem*. These still would *not* be preventive measures, although intervention in cases of less-than-severe involvement has a way of getting called prevention. (That is only prevention of severe involvement, not prevention of the disorder.)

Prevention requires a fairly systematic and comprehensive program to block or reduce—prevent—the actual development of the disorder. With coronaries, the goal is a reduction in the *occurrence* of heart attacks by attention to high vulnerability indices. The goal is not really to have better means of treatment *after* the heart muscle is damaged, although that can certainly be a by-product. The goal is to achieve a record of fewer coronaries per 100,000 people at risk, by utilizing a true preventive system.

The high-risk concept in alcohol work is exactly analogous; it has been in use and is already demonstrating itself to have great value.

When I talk about these high-risk concepts in front of groups I always announce that I will certainly offend everyone in the audience or his parents before I'm through.

The "addictive personality" is at high risk for future alcohol involvement. Persons who get on "kicks" of any kind— particularly of foods, drinks, or chemicals—are said to have addictive personalities. I can perhaps speak with some authority on this subject, as I am definitely an addictive kind of character. I smoke cigarettes. I drink a fair amount of coffee. I go on kicks of a certain flavor or brand of candy. I love Coca-Cola for a while, and then I'll switch to Kool-Aid or peanut-butter sandwiches. I'm even "kicky" on what I read.

Look in on an AA meeting. There's a lot of coffee, and you could walk on the cigarette smoke. The meeting is, after all, a gathering of addictive personalities. I am not being accusatory, nor can I afford to point a finger, since I share that addictive tendency.

Just in passing, in many treatment, detoxification, or other rehabilitation facilities for alcohol troubled people ample coffee is available. Coffee is a powerful social habit and is very often a valuable therapeutic tool. And it's civilized, too.

But in such facilities, including the general medical hospital, it is not unusual for people coming off alcohol to have as many as twenty to thirty cups of coffee daily. The helper must be very careful to check the caffeine intake of each resident, particularly the individual who begins to get shaky, tremulous, and nervous all over again after two to five days of acute withdrawal. These people will often begin to request sleeping medication, tranquilizers, and special personal attention. Under such circumstances it is wise to ask how much coffee he or she is drinking daily.

You don't ordinarily have to be wary of false responses —it usually suffices to describe the likely outcome of too much coffee and ask the patient to hold it to about five cups maximum per day. Alcohol-involved people are (in this as in much else) very like everyone else—surprised that the coffee might make them more uncomfortable than necessary and quite reasonable and agreeable about cutting back when alerted.

It is a truism in alcohol work that one watches carefully for chemical overuse—whether it be caffeine or something else, because we are dealing constantly with people who are likely to be of an addictive bent even before they start drinking.

Anyone who, because of his or her easily addictable nature, is already involved in chemicals in general is at high risk for future alcohol involvement. Some persons in alcohol work have become terror-stricken by the effect on potential and current alcohol abusers of the muscle relaxant and tranquilizer Valium. Valium is an extremely useful medication when prescribed with appropriate care and knowledge of its effects. It is not necessary to argue about its usefulness— it is clearly a helpful drug when properly employed. Valium, however, is extremely dangerous for people vulnerable to alcohol troubles. Valium seems to "zonk out" such people, to give them a "high" and an immediate and striking reduction of anxiety very similar to the effects derived from alcohol. It can lead to poor judgment, depression, and confusion.

Since Valium is in such widespread and uncritical use,

it is not unusual to run into alcohol troubled persons who frankly say that since their discovery of Valium they have no "need" for alcohol.

I recall a man who went to a pretty good alcohol treatment facility, and while taking time out for this he decided to take care of some of his physical problems as well, among which was a bad back for which he underwent spinal fusion. To reduce the muscle spasms and pain, his surgeon prescribed Valium, and the man then became intoxicated on that. He was "high," had slurred speech, staggered, and so on. He was convinced that he was sober, because he was not drinking alcohol, and when the Valium was withdrawn he immediately began drinking again, making a "decision" in one confused state to go back to his other form of "high."

The effects of the two chemicals in alcohol-vulnerable people are so similar that if you find, in taking a history, that a person has been on Valium other than temporarily— even if prescribed, and even if prescribed originally for a good reason—the odds are very high that if the person is not an ATP he or she is at high risk for becoming one. If he likes what Valium does, just wait until he finds alcohol as a "trouble-dissolver"!

Included in the high-risk category is anyone who is on Valium for too long and/or is on it, without complaining, at a dosage higher than 5 milligrams three times a day.

Another illustrative story: I had an appointment with a man and his wife whom I had last seen four and a half years earlier. Bob was a severe and chronic ATP whom AA had helped a great deal. About a month before, he had become seriously drunk for about eight or nine hours, having been sober since I had last seen him. Three weeks later he drank again.

He reported (as if it made some useful difference to either of us, which it didn't) that he didn't like to drink anymore and wasn't drinking in his old compulsive way. I quickly assured him that his reasons for drinking again were not very important right now. Then I noticed that he had a very definite feel of depression about him, and I was uncomfortably surprised to realize that he had felt that way to me before and I had somehow not picked it up and dealt with it.

Bob's wife had called for the meeting—not, she said, because he had started drinking again (although I'm sure that was part of it), but because in the years of his sobriety their uncommunicative, unrewarding relationship had not improved, and the children had become unhappy and begun to develop school and behavior problems.

She wanted some marital counseling, and he had agreed to come with her so that they could see me as a couple. She felt, and he agreed, that in addition to the alcohol problem they had some other problems they needed to work on.

I could accept that, if we agreed to deal with the alcohol problem too. Bob's apparent depression bothered me, and I asked him if he were "a little bit depressed" and if he thought we might consider that to be part of our business. He reacted with surprise—had he himself never used that word for it, or was I the first person to ask him about it?—and with some relief that it was now out front. "A little?" said he. "I'm so goddamned depressed I don't know what to do, and I've been that way for years!"

To make the final point, I must provide some background. I had recently written about the dangers of Valium and had been told that an alcohol-Valium research proposal I had conceived and initiated had probably received federal funding. The purpose of the research was to investigate and demonstrate scientifically the dangers of the alcohol-Valium combination.

Also, a few weeks earlier, I had given a final examination in an undergraduate class and had asked a question about the dangers of the same alcohol-Valium combination. Those corrected exams were on a chair outside my office when I arrived a little late for my appointment with Bob and his wife, and he looked at the exam while waiting.

I was wondering what made me so uncomfortable about

his depression and the fact that I had missed it years before when in retrospect it had been there right along. Having seen the examination item, Bob asked about Valium and alcohol. I spoke very strongly to the effect that it was poison to alcohol troubled people, that they sometimes got confused, or depressed, or zonked-out with it, that they tended to overdo or stay on it for too long, and that it was in fact a good index for locating people who might in the future have problems.

A pause. "I've been on it for nine years. I never knew that."

I couldn't believe it. Now I would have to get him off that, probably on an antidepressant for a while (contrary to some opinion, not *all* medication is bad for such people), and then his utter fatigue and inability to deal with himself and his wife and kids would have a real chance to improve.

So we parted with great optimism. I was *very* hopeful about Bob and about his relationship with his wife, but wondering somewhat about the level of my own brilliance.

But my story isn't over. Bob, I discovered, was very friendly with Bill, the man who went on Valium after his back operation. Bob, it developed, was the one who got Bill off the Valium, on grounds that it wasn't good for alcoholics! We laughed together, I a little ruefully.

Barbiturates are closely related to alcohol in both pharmacological and psychological effects. Not surprisingly, the two are often used in combination by chemical abusers. In the barbiturate family are many sleeping preparations and medications to relieve anxieties. Unfortunately, the barbiturates, like alcohol, are highly addicting and have many of the same negative effects as alcohol.

It appears, in fact, that one can build up a cross-tolerance to alcohol by taking too many barbiturates, and vice versa. Thus, without ever touching alcohol, one can build up a tolerance to it via barbiturates. Conversely, alcohol withdrawal symptoms can be alleviated by substitution of barbiturates.

The oft-reported deaths attributed to overdoses of sleeping pills are quite often due to a combination of alcohol and barbiturates. The victims take a few drinks, then a couple of pills, then a couple more drinks, and pretty soon they can't remember what they've taken. So they take some more of each, and pretty soon they're dead.

Persons with a history of alcohol problems in the immediate family—among parents or siblings, for example—are at high risk for future alcohol problems. The family variable has two facets, both of which revolve around the notion that one cannot be raised in a family with an ATP in it and retain a moderate view toward alcohol.

Thus, some people from such families of origin are immoderate in their opposition to, and fear of, alcohol. This is most likely to be the case if the ATP parent had almost nothing in his personal makeup to draw the child toward his or her values. Thus, a clearly little-loved mother, in her cups most of the time, ineffectual and obnoxious, is not likely to stimulate any real identification. Her child is then pretty safe from booze.

On the other hand, it is quite difficult to find an ATP who offers *nothing* good, supportive, or protective toward his or her children, or who never has. Alcohol troubled people are often potentially charming, bright, and well-meaning underneath it all. When they are parents, they throw their kids into the high-risk pool, because in the process of identification the child finds so much worthwhile about the parent that he cannot reject all the parent's characteristics and values.

The concept of identification can be explained briefly like this: If it pays a child in some substantial fashion to believe as the parent believes, the child is likely to do so. The child is then said to identify with the parent and the parent's values. If the parent cannot make it pay, the child will reject the notions and the parent.

Thus, offspring occasionally leave the family nest quite early and do not return—either physically or emotionally. Children leave for reasons other than rejection, of course. Mobility in the United States is high; job opportunities may exist in a distant location; children cast their lot with their spouses and careers, and so on. But the kid who essentially runs away from home and neither maintains nor reestablishes psychological contact has not identified adequately.

Parents are at least for a time much stronger than their kids, a situation that produces the peculiar but not uncommon "identification with the aggressor" or "lining up with the winner." It was through this kind of identification that Adolf Hitler was able, under particular cultural circumstances, to draw to himself large numbers of people afraid to be either winners or losers on their own.

Observe the kids at summer camp, or in college, or in graduate school, feeling picked on during initiation rites, becoming counselors or teachers in later years and doing the same thing to the next generation; they bought the strength of the top dog, who gave them something in return—protection. But if there is merely strength or aggression and no payoff, then there will be little or no identification.

So with the alcohol troubled parent. When you're a kid he may beat up and terrorize the whole family on payday, but if you're insecure enough and if he doesn't hit you if you don't get in his way when he's beating up other people you will learn how to act to remain safe—and in the process pick up his value system. That's identification with the aggressor. If he beats you up no matter *what* you do, there's no payoff and you don't need him.

There's another kind of identification, too—usually a more positive one. It is initially connected with the protection of a stronger person, but it also has a life of its own —this is the payoff of being loved and accepted, and of being protected and given security on that basis. The idea of identification, however it occurs, means that the one identifying takes on *for himself* the ideas and values of the model.

Imagine a girl growing up in a family in which the mother (protecting and loving in many ways) handles family and personal crises by getting migraine headaches. Obviously the woman's daughter (probably more than a son, because the daughter is more likely to have a role similar to her mother's) is at risk of producing migraines in her own later life. If the mother is not loved or respected by the daughter, however, the girl will have only scorn for others who have migraines. Perhaps she will snort and say, "My mother used to avoid life that way. Not me!"

In the case of migraines, as of alcohol, it is not necessary for the learner to learn on purpose or to be aware of what is happening. In some cases the learner may have a physiological predisposition, although in my opinion that is a small factor. It must be kept in mind that the migrainous mother never herself learned ways of handling her anger in a way more effective than migraines; in the case of the ATP, he or she never learned a better way of handling anxiety. How, then, could he teach it to his children?

If a boy, then, has a father who is in trouble with alcohol but who nevertheless has qualities worth emulating, that boy is at high risk for alcohol troubles. Is the father a pretty good lawyer? Or truck driver, farmer, or carpenter? Or an effective, well-liked, rollicking, John Wayne-type, masculine brawler? The son is at risk.

I am reminded of the client who, at twenty-six, had an alcohol troubled mother who lived in a city housing project. She had been married four times and was, as far as I could tell, almost completely unrewarding to her son, whom we will call John. He, having been deprived of most good things in his early life, was in love with the fantasy of the "good fairy godmother," and kept acting as if his mother would turn into one if only he put up with her for long enough.

Now John had temporal lobe epilepsy, so when he either

drank or came under strong stress he would blank out and lose the ability to recall what he had done—he became, in fact, an automatic robot. Very early in my contact with him a fortunate thing happened. John was picked up by the police after a telephone call from the mother that a man was stalking her in the shrubbery outside her first-floor apartment. It was John, not intoxicated at the moment but just coming off, in a temporal lobe automatism. He was indulging in a little game of Guadacanal, fully equipped to do his mother in, and quite genuinely unable, when he came out of it, to recall or believe what he had done. Consciously he was aware only of some annoyance at his mother's constant querulous demands for him to pay more attention to her, hang her curtains, fetch her beer, and so on.

Among other things, what we did with John was break his dependence on his mother by helping him see that she had never been, was not, and never would be a "real mother" and that his identification with her (or acceptance of her values as his own) was built on a poor trade. "Would you," I asked, "spend any time with this person if she were not named Mother? Is there something about her as a person that gives you a payoff or ever did? Or is she simply a person who happened to get pregnant and then delivered you? Did she then behave toward you as you would wish a mother to do?"

We meet John again later in this chapter. Very rewarding guy.

All the foregoing is a long-winded way of showing that the children (or siblings, because they are raised under similar family value systems) of alcohol troubled people are at high risk for later alcohol abuse—if, as is very often the case, the parent had something either good or powerful to offer.

In any event, we do not expect a balanced, moderate view toward alcohol from the offspring of alcohol troubled people. We find instead people who are immoderate in one direction or the other, depending in part on the extent to which they were able to identify with the troubled parent.

At one extreme are the ones who can see none of the pleasant uses of alcohol. Frightened and hurt by the parent's misuse of it, they become prudish teetotalers. At the other extreme, of course, are those who tend to misuse alcohol themselves: "If it was good enough for my father it's good enough for me."

Neither group is balanced or moderate—they represent the extremes.

All this should give parents something to ponder. The alcohol troubled parent is putting his or her children in danger of serious problems. During a child's formative years one is dealing not only with whether or not the child's life is as good as possible at the moment, but more importantly with the groundwork that is being laid for when he is thirty or forty. Parents may not realize that they can implant a time bomb in their children and set it to go off twenty-five years later when they're not even around. The diabolical unpleasantry about all this lies in the paradox that if the parent doesn't really care about the child he or she is likely to be so poor a model that the kid is fairly safe anyway. But if the parent in some way commands love or respect the risk of implanting the time bomb is immeasurably increased.

If you're a parent who is drinking too much, you must realize that Fate doesn't care much about your good intentions. While it is something of a truism in alcohol work that you give it up for yourself, there are exceptions. This is one of the exceptions. You don't want to be a time-bomber of your kids, do you?

People from families in which alcohol is the preferred or routine social lubricant are at high risk for alcohol troubles. Many alcohol-involved people and their spouses have difficulty believing a simple truth—a large segment of our population routinely offers coffee, tea, or a soft drink rather than alcohol to visitors in their homes. That, as a matter of fact, is the kind of home I was raised in, and it is the custom in my present home. Some of our friends do likewise, and others routinely offer alcohol. The reason is not basically financial (although certain youthful members of the family refer to me as "El Cheapo") but simply that it does not occur to me to offer alcohol. We have it, and sometimes use it, and throw drinking parties now and again. But unless the occasion is labeled a cocktail party I do not think of it unless the visitors are of Italian extraction—I have finally learned that then it is good manners to remember the wine.

I am aware that my forgetfulness, or my failure to be programmed this way, has sometimes seemed rude or inhospitable to others—to someone from an alcohol-offering background my behavior must seem inexcusable.

The point remains: If your family of origin values alcohol as a gift from host to visitor, your risk is increased.

People from certain ethnic or religious subcultures are at high risk for alcohol troubles.   At risk in decreasing order among religious groups are Catholics, Protestants, Jews, Muslims, and adherents to the major Eastern religions. And some specific ethnic groups are at very high risk.

In the geographical area where I do most of my work the Irish Catholic is at massive risk into about the third or fourth generation. This is apparently particularly true of the male, although the women, perhaps as they become acculturated to a slightly less male-oriented world, are probably catching up. In any event, females of Irish descent are also at quite high risk.

An Irish-American patient of mine once told me of a wake he attended. The deceased had died as a direct consequence of his alcohol-induced cirrhotic liver. His grandmother, watching the survivors getting bombed, sighed and said, "It's in the blud!"

Well, it's not in the "blud" but learned, and as we get further from the Irish subculture and its attitudes toward alcohol the problem seems to ease off.

Many facets of the Irish society and the economics of the Ould Sod have contributed. Historically, in order to maintain farm holdings large enough to support families even barely adequately, the oldest son by custom inherited. The other sons eventually either left the land or ended up working for their eldest brother, and the daughters, of course, could never inherit.

There was, however, a chronological fly in the ointment. As the parents became older and less active the children also matured and, in the nature of things, had little economic reason to be held to the land they could never inherit. It would be natural for them to leave, but it was clearly not in the best interests of the aging parents to lose their labor force too early.

The mother, filled with ambivalence herself, was therefore extremely charming yet also controlling. The sons were held by her very real warmth and yet driven away from her, and from women, by the strength and agility of her control. The pub therefore developed for men only, and in American inner-city bars the Irish still do not drink with their women. It is a place of sanctuary from them.

So the Irish male leaves his family of origin late and marries late, but only after he has developed a taste for male camaraderie in the pub. He associates the ability to hold his liquor with masculinity, and even the alcohol-tinged fights are occasions for conviviality and good fellowship. Who can forget the glorious battle in *The Quiet Man*, in which the two great alcoholic bull mooses, Victor McLaglen and John Wayne, collide in prodigious battle, only to pick one another up and arm-in-arm proceed to the local pub— great friends?

Despite the crescendoes on Saturday nights, pay nights, election nights, promotion nights, wakes, weddings, and St. Paddy's Day, the Irish-American alcohol-involved individual tends to be a nibbler, a constant nipper, maintaining some level of alcohol in his blood much of the time. In this he is relatively unlike his Slavic counterpart, who is likely to drink more sporadically and explosively.

The female, even unto the third and fourth generation in this country, tends to be alternately warm and punitively controlling. The Irish male raised by this traditional mother figure tends to retain family loyalties and responsibilities very long, to have considerable mixed feelings about women, and to marry late. More of his sisters devote their lives to the aging, sick, or widowed mother than is the case in the general population. The family elects one daughter to tend the mother while the rest of the children go to work, get married, and contribute financial and emotional support.

And they have alcohol troubles—as nurses, lawyers, police, and firemen.

I heard a story from a man who was once standing with the Irish owner of a New York City bar frequented almost exclusively by lads of Irish descent. The owner said, "Look at them all snuggled up to that bar. They all look alike and they drink about the same. We're not running a bar here. We're running an Irish death wish!"

The American Indian, too, is traditionally at terribly high risk. He ritually went into the wilderness and starved himself until he had hallucinations. He developed a religion around peyote and other hallucinogens. Popular wisdom is that the red man cannot handle firewater. There is no particular reason to believe that he inherits alcohol-vulnerable genes, but as long as he holds Indian cultural beliefs he is at high risk.

The white man won this country from its original owners not with guns but with the drug alcohol, with which he made the Indian sick and ineffectual. Firewater, not firearms.

Slavs also are at high risk, mainly while they are in cultural transition, but not especially so as they become acculturated. When at high risk, they tend to be explosive binge drinkers.

Jews are at low risk until they get acculturated; as

they lose the supporting structure of the Hebrew tradition, in which it's fine to drink but never to the point of losing control of oneself, their risk rate rises to meet that of the general population. Increasing numbers of young Jewish people, again about third generation, are in trouble with alcohol.

French-Canadians are at rather high risk, having a pattern of both frequent nibbling and exploding.

WASPs, White Anglo-Saxon Protestants, seem to be at relatively high risk, particularly if they are upper-middle-class or higher. They, too, tend to be nibblers, but not open, gregarious, honest ones like the Irish. Rather, they are inclined to be secretive and relatively well-bred and controlled.

Italians tend to be rather regular and heavy consumers of alcohol but generate only a low to medium trouble rate, apparently due to the subcultural controls, which value the ability to function over the sheer consumption of alcohol, and due also to their interest in food. Alcohol to the Italian is not supposed to replace food but to complement it; it is in fact as much a food as a drink.

Muslims, whether black or Middle Eastern, are forbidden by religious law to use alcohol and are thus at low risk, as are Orientals.

Blacks, particularly but not exclusively young urban males, are at high risk for alcohol troubles, as for other chemical usage. There appears to be a built-in subcultural strength in black society, however, that somehow makes it more possible than among whites for the middle-aged black who has been in genuine trouble for many years to give up alcohol. Whether this assertion can be supported scientifically is still to be tested. There is no question of high risk, and no question that many young blacks die or get damaged with alcohol. But a "street" observation strongly suggests that at the age when the average chronic and severe white alcohol troubled male starts a swift downward slide (age forty-five-plus), a surprising number of black males are able to grab hold of themselves. The young, drinking males often refer to their fathers' or uncles' giving it up.

It may be that the black community has a strength in this regard that will hold up under scrutiny and help us all in our efforts to find useful systems of change. Or perhaps the observation is confined to the relatively small northeastern city we have begun to check out. The black leaders in this community seem to agree; in any event, so far we can simply say that something positive seems to happen.

Although the sheer rate of alcohol troubles is high among blacks, it is like a stream that disappears. We do not in general find blacks in proportional numbers at the end of the alcohol conduits—alcoholic deaths, general hospital wards, AA, private rehabilitation facilities, state mental hospitals, hospitals for chronic diseases, mental hygiene clinics.

The reason may be that our society often uses differential socioeconomic and racial standards in application of the civil laws. Since the prisons are disproportionately populated by blacks, it may be that, although we do not find blacks in the usual alcohol conduits, they are "hidden" in the prison system.

No socioeconomic class or racial, ethnic, or religious group gets off scot-free as far as booze is concerned, but some, it is clear, are at much higher risk than others. We are not being insulting or putting any group down in this regard, nor is there evidence of hereditary taint. Some subcultures, statistically, protect their members better against alcohol than others do. Conversely, some of our subcultures, by means of social training and expectations, put their members at great hazard.

People in certain occupations seem to be at high risk for alcohol troubles. It is hard to sort out which comes first, the booze problem or the kind of job that will nurture the problem in its origin and growth. Any job not requiring regular hours and supervision is likely to have a high population of alcohol-prone individuals in it. For example, alcohol troubles are often especially well hidden in the housewife if she is vulnerable.

Taxi drivers have traditionally had a high rate of alcohol involvement—their hours are long but tend to be unsupervised and irregular. In many cities, the cabbie's references are not checked—it is not a high-paying job and there is considerable turnover. The job provides latitude for the recovering—or sliding—severe ATP to function.

House painters also work irregular hours. Like the taxi driver, they have long hours when they work, but they are relatively unsupervised. Painters also have breaks between jobs, between seasons, due to weather, and so forth.

Salesmen, especially if they travel, also tend to be at high risk, again because of irregular supervision, and also perhaps because of an additional hazard—the let's-do-business-over-a-drink social custom.

To the extent that the hard-driving businessman or lawyer feels impelled to do business over a drink, his risk factor, too, is raised. These people tend to be self-employed and gregarious. It is apparent that some people from these categories are protected from the late-lunch martinis by the value systems of their subcultures—others are not so protected.

Anyone who has worked in the field attempting to make a first engagement, an initial involving contact with alcohol troubled people, will recall many individuals who cannot imagine being successful businessmen if the cocktail meeting—which they consider one of the essential tools of their trade—is denied them.

This mixing of alcohol with business matters is a deeply ingrained custom in our society. In a place where I have worked, one can always tell that internal, interpersonal difficulties have arisen in the organization when notices go up that there will be a "wine and cheese" get-together on Friday night at so-and-so's house. Somehow there is an implication that we can always work out our difficulties as we get cheerfully relaxed together.

At another place, where I worked as a consultant setting up what turned out to be an excellent alcohol program, I attended a staff Christmas party. The program was about a year old, and much of the year's effort had been directed toward educating and informing physicians, nurses, health aides, and administrators to early identification, treatment, and prevention efforts with alcohol troubled people, and to help them deal even with moderate and severe problems in their patient contacts. The party involved all these people.

Much progress had been made—yet the purchase of a ticket to the party automatically gave one a chance on the door prize—a large and generous basket of booze! The incongruity became momentarily embarrassing when the young and dedicated psychologist who was heading the alcohol program won the prize. We had been discussing its inappropriateness when his name was announced. He's the kind of guy who is capable of refusing to accept under such circumstances, yet what can one do at a Christmas party? Grin and bear it, I suppose, and then back to the old drawing board.

Obviously, our society generates very strong and real social pressures to drink. These can be overcome very comfortably when the individual makes up his mind to not drink. Business can be conducted without joining the drinking. Contracts can be drawn up, closings can be celebrated, mergers toasted, even in a drinking group by the individual who no longer drinks alcohol.

The stratagems are many and varied—all are based on a firm and active decision to *not* drink, come hell or high water, pestilence, fire, or death. I like to see people say straight out, "I can't drink." There is no logical requirement that they add, "I'm in trouble with alcohol" or "I am an alcoholic." But if one feels impelled to volunteer that information there is no major objection to it.

My friend Ambrose, noted with deep affection and respect in the dedication, sometimes used the Shirley Temple
ploy. He arranged with the bartender to make him a Shirley Temple—a nonalcoholic drink filled with garbage to
make it look like an exotic cocktail—when the drinks were
served. I'm not sure why he did this—everyone knew he
was a brilliant physician who had lost his practice because
of booze. He had no ambivalence whatever about drinking
versus not drinking—I saw him go through excruciating
dental pain rather than take medication that he thought
might get him drinking again. Maybe the Shirley Temples
were out of courtesy to his Hibernian chums whom he did
not wish to make uncomfortable.

Others use some variant of the "My doctor says I
can't" ploy. Although I prefer the straight "I can't drink"
statement, I am not knocking anything that is comfortable
and works. "I have high blood pressure" is excellent, as is
"My doctor says I have to lose weight" or "My ulcer has
been kicking up" or "It's bad for my migraines."

Nothing works if the ATP hasn't made the tough decision. *Anything* works when the decision is made, whether
the pressures are social or business ones.

I mentioned John before, stalking his mother. He was
the father of four little kids, unemployed, on welfare, living
in a housing project, flaky, and subject to temporal lobe
seizures. Whenever he went to his wife's brother's house
John would start drinking again. After each incident, he
would complain that the brother-in-law would not take no
for an answer. We talked about that, dealing with whether
or not and to what extent he himself had made a decision—
obviously, the decision should not properly be left to the
brother-in-law.

Eventually John came in to report to me, with smiling
pride all over his face, the following incident:

The brother-in-law had pressed him to take a drink.
"No, thank you," said John as usual. "You know I can't
drink."

"Well, just one won't hurt you," said the brother-in-law, also as usual.

"All right," said John, as usual. "But if I'm going off the wagon, give me some of that good scotch, and make it strong."

The drink was duly poured, and John asked that it be thickened a bit. Then he held it to the light. "I'll be damned, there's a fly in it," said he, and poured it down the sink. "Give me another, just like that, but make it a little stronger."

After the third fly had been discovered and poured down the drain, the brother-in-law looked at John and said, "You really mean it, don't you?"

I confess that I was as proud as John was. He's made it so far, and that was eight years ago.

A summary of the high-risk category seems to require a statement that (1) although some kinds of people are at higher risk than others, no one is absolutely safe and (2) the high-risk notion is important because it provides a beginning *preventive* effort rather than solely a rehabilitation effort.

6
The Numbers Game

From some we loved, the
Loveliest and the best
That from his Vintage rolling
Time hath prest,
Have drunk their Cup a
Round or two before,
And one by one crept
Silently to rest.

The Rubaiyat of Omar Khayam

No discussion of the alcohol issue is complete without a discussion of the dimensions of the problem. Ever since, years ago, I read a little book called *How to Lie With Statistics*, I have looked a bit askance at the world of numbers. Over the years I have learned something about statistics—how they are gathered, manipulated, and shaped. There is a saying in the world of computers, "garbage in, garbage out," which means simply that if you insert data collected in a biased or selective way your computer will end up giving you clean-looking numbers based on untruths. Happens all the time.

163

The fact that current estimates of the number of alcoholics in the United States are variously between four and twenty million may make little impression one way or the other. At least it never did on me. Then when I learned that not everyone agrees on what an alcoholic is, or on whether an "alcoholic" is any different from a problem drinker, I began to have more trouble about numbers.

If you are in alcohol difficulties or are about to be, there is little earthly use in knowing about such big numbers except for what small comfort you derive out of having company in your misery. It *is* useful to know that large numbers of people will recover from, or "arrest," their problem, and that you can certainly become one of them.

If your man, or child, or wife, or parent has difficulties in this area it is perhaps of relatively little use to learn that alcohol problems so far tend to develop quite silently—they are poorly visible to most people until they are well past the serious trouble stage. Clearly, we have even greater numbers in trouble than we have publicized, and also a greater improvement rate.

It is popular in alcohol circles to multiply the number of so-called "alcoholics" (whoever they may be, because one man's alcoholic is another man's life of the party) by a constant number, say 3.5. This constant is the number of people, usually in the troubled person's family, who are supposed to be affected by the drinker's foolishness. So if we multiply 14 million by 3.5 we end up with 49 million, or about one-fourth of our population. It may well be true, but who cares? All you really need to know is that alcohol is a huge problem and possibly that it can be relatively silent and insidious and that it affects most sufferers minimally or moderately rather than severely.

I was once asked to help construct an "alcohol grant"—an application for federal funding by a large and excellent general medical hospital. In discussing the shape of the grant, why the project should be funded, and so on, it seemed appropriate to give some numbers.

The atmosphere of the meeting was affected by the fact that most of the people in the room were high-powered physicians and hospital administrators who were, in fact, extremely unknowledgeable about alcohol. I felt it would be against the best interests of the grant to give the real figures. (In repeated surveys on general medical and surgical wards in city hospitals, it is revealed that somewhere around 40 to 60 percent of the adult beds are filled with persons with alcohol-associated problems.)

I gave the figure as "at least 40 percent." Eyebrows went up; I heard a murmur of disbelief; and it became clear that, even while reducing the figure, I had lost some credibility with my audience, except for the nurse-practitioners, who nodded.

I demonstrated ways they could plug alcohol problems into their multiphasic screening system (which had at that time no alcohol-related items). I suggested, for example, that if they received a case of combined malnutrition and pneumonia, the likelihood of significant alcohol involvement was very high. As explained earlier, the same goes for any combination of pneumonia, broken bones, malnutrition, gastrectomy scars (from surgery for ulcers), feelings of impending doom, and/or tuberculosis. Thus, if an individual comes to a hospital with a history of gastrectomy and TB, look for alcohol. You will not always be right, but your hit rate will be high. Persons in trouble with alcohol will react to knowledgeable alcohol-oriented questions by the physician in revealing ways—hesitations, evasions, overstatements, and so forth.

Three months after this meeting I received an excited call from one of the physicians, informing me that they were up to "45 percent already." I suggested he keep looking—that the rate might go higher.

Probably about 60 percent of first admissions to mental hospitals are alcohol-associated. Half of our highway fatalities are. Half of our troubled people in general may be, although the average community mental hygiene clinic is oriented toward "psychotic" or "neurotic" or "depressed" people and is quite lacking in useful sensitivity to minimal, moderate, or even severe instances of alcohol damage.

If you throw a net out into a community by saying, "All of you in trouble, come to us, whether with financial, childrearing, marital, employment, physical, emotional, or other problems," you will catch in your net a group of whom 50 percent or more have alcohol-related troubles. It's been done.

Family and domestic relations courts also hover about the 50 percent mark. Most of the people who come into contact with alcohol troubled individuals are neither attuned to nor informed about the problem. Nor can they define what an alcoholic is, in general, beyond some kind of ridiculous "skid row" observation.

In attempting to inform such people (who tend to come from nondrinking subcultures) of the dimensions of the problem, alcohol-wise persons should sometimes deemphasize so the listener will hear at least some of the message. No one listens to someone who sounds too much like a crusader.

Alcohol workers may be tempted to inflate numbers by throwing into the category "alcoholic" as many hard-core cases as possible. Paradoxically, this is neither the most convincing, the most truthful, nor the most inflating way to demonstrate the immensity of the problem. The best and most realistic way, for manifold reasons discussed elsewhere, is simply to include people who have troubles generated by the use of alcohol. By and large those are not the individuals generally called "alcoholic," yet there are vastly greater numbers of them.

Since between four and twenty million people are in alcohol difficulties as defined in the restrictive "chronic alcoholic" sense, the fact that Alcoholics Anonymous claims membership of about three-quarters of a million is impressive. It is the single most involved unit dealing with the issue, yet one must note the huge unengaged alcohol troubled population remaining. In my little state of Rhode Island it is said that there are 40,000 alcoholics; AA claims membership here of about 2,500.

Interest in doing more, and doing it better, for the alcohol sufferer is growing rapidly. This can mean reaching a greater proportion of hard-core, severely damaged individuals and providing more and better facilities for them, and it should also come to mean developing better identification, outreach, and preventive systems.

The odds against recovery can be considered overwhelming or optimistic, depending on the population. To reach 10 or 15 percent with skid row bums is a mark of real excellence in a program. Again, success depends to some extent on how one conceptualizes the issues—a "rule of 10 percent" appears to operate with such severely damaged people. For example, any given treatment course with such people has about a 10 percent chance of success over the length of the one attempt. (Say it's a trial in a halfway house.) The second attempt also delivers a 10 percent opportunity. You consider these 10 percent chances separately, not cumulatively. These are very rough approximations, of course, with many exceptions and mitigating circumstances.

You can also generally assume that you can add a 10 percent chance of improvement for each honest-to-goodness strength in either the ATP or his environment. A helpful (not necessarily sympathetic) wife, a clergyman who knows his business regarding alcohol, an employer who wants to help, or a job to return to all qualify in this regard. Here we can cumulate—10 percent plus 10 percent plus 10 percent equals 30 percent.

But the basic figure on which you build, and the expectation with which you start, is a grim 10 percent outlook for severely damaged individuals.

On the other hand, to help only 50 percent constitutes failure in a population of ATPs who have had the problem a short time, who have no criminal record, whose bodies and brains are undamaged, or who retain careers, families, and emotional stability. In populations of this variety—people with a great deal going for them and in minimal to moderate (but real) trouble, we can expect a 75 to 85 percent hit rate in a good program. Again, per course of treatment.

But always remember what is in back of the numbers—in the last analysis they should measure what they stand for. For example, adding severely impaired people into the same statistics as minimally troubled people is to add two different things, the old apples and oranges fallacy.

To compare the outcome of Happy Valley Farm, the fancy treatment retreat house, with the outcome of the local state hospital is not enlightening because Happy Valley may be failing to deliver a good percentage figure (say, only 45 percent), while the state hospital alcohol ward is delivering 15 percent. For the severely damaged state hospital population that might be a superb job.

In short, I mistrust the ways numbers are collected and shaped to prove one point or another. Even if I could select the statistics, assumptions, and definitions that were acceptable to my sense of fairness and honesty and rule out those that were generated to justify a higher budget for a certain agency next year, most of the numbers would still leave me cold, as I suspect is the case with most people.

It should suffice to say that in alcohol work we are concerned with absolutely *huge* numbers, to emphasize that we have very good reason to believe that about half of our citizens in substantial life difficulties have alcohol-related troubles, and then to attempt to make the enormities somehow visible to the alerted eye in everyday life.

One way for me to do this is to note the problems, with people I know, in my neighborhood and community. I register these things all the time—deaths, arrests, hospitalizations, lost jobs, and broken homes. Yet I realize I am, by training and experience, more alert than most.

Somehow the numbers situation is nowhere more evident to me than in the alcohol-related trash along our highways, and I don't see any legitimate way to transform that multitude of annual tons to numbers. There is general agreement that alcohol and automobiles constitute a bad combination; every spring I am newly appalled to see windrows of beer cans, whiskey bottles, and other assorted alcohol containers as they emerge from the melting snowbanks. I never can believe it, and this particular statistic, which has no number attached to it, becomes symbolic to me of the sheer massiveness of the problem. I do not mean to be shallow or superficial when I say that this visual slum seems to have more impact on us than do the death and destruction of individual human beings and of families. Perhaps it is because we do not actually see them so clearly—and we are so used to having large, meaningless numbers pressed on us.

I have been experimenting on my acquaintances to determine whether piles of beer cans impress them as they do me, and the initial returns suggest that I should ask you to look at the highways in your area in order to get a good idea of numbers.

7
Alcoholics Anonymous

Before I found AA, I tried everything. Doctors, shrinks, clergy—everything. None of them did me a damned bit of good. Only AA showed me how to solve my problem.
An anonymous alcoholic

In the relatively brief time since alcoholism has become an "accepted" social and medical problem, a curiously ambivalent set of attitudes has developed between many— probably most—members of the oldest and strongest self-help agency, Alcoholics Anonymous, and the small army of non-alcoholic professionals and paraprofessionals now working in the field.

In badly over-simplified form, the two attitudes might be summarized this way:

AA: We are the only people who have the real answer to our common problem. Non-alcoholics, no matter what their training nor how good their intentions, are at best useless and at worst downright harmful.

The professionals: AA may be minimally helpful and should be tolerated and humored, but its chief value is to relieve us of responsibility for the problem of alcoholism in general and those aspects of it that we don't care to tackle in particular.

It is impossible to be around AA for very long without hearing the familiar litany of the unique power of this fellowship. Rare indeed is the AA member with the self-understanding and perception to say, as one did at an AA meeting recently, "Before I came to AA, I tried everything. Doctors, hospitals, psychiatrists, psychologists, social workers, churches, and *every one* of them helped me—they all prepared me to accept and use AA."

There are reasons for the prevailing AA attitude, reasons which the non-alcoholic worker in the field needs to understand. These are some of them:

1. AA was, after all, first out of the gate. Its members were hard at work trying to help themselves and each other long before most professionals took any interest in their problem. Inevitably, it has established a track record of which its members are justly, if often inordinately, proud.

2. Many AA members will never forget the stigma that society (including representatives of the professions recently become active in the field) long attached, and frequently still attaches, to their problem. It is easy to transfer this resentment to "do-gooders" now trying to "help."

3. More than a few AA members have indeed suffered from ignorance and misguided advice at the hands of some professional people. A common AA lament recounts experiences with medical doctors, psychiatrists, and others who counseled various sorts of "restraint" and "self-control." Too often and too readily, such experience translates into suspicion and rejection of all professional assistance.

Prejudice against AA among the professionals probably is not so prevalent nor so deep-seated as the opposite attitude. And it seems a safe generalization that the more direct experience professionals and para-professionals have with alcoholism and alcoholics, the easier it is for them to understand and deal with AA crotchets, and to exploit intelligently AA's unquestionable strengths. The greater need is for other and more professional people in all fields to recognize their stake, like society's, in helping to combat the problem. Far too common still are professionals who are quite willing to take AA at what seems to be its own self-evaluation as the one true road and to "let AA handle it."

But the truth is that AA cannot handle it alone. For relatively few alcoholics is it really the sole answer. If treatment of alcoholism may be divided into three broad phases—detoxification, education, and maintenance—then it follows that AA is of minimal help in the first phase, of moderate help in the second, and of maximal (but rarely complete) help in the third. More professionals and more AAers alike must be brought to see this.

Something of a microcosm of the prevailing ambivalence may be seen in the attitudes toward what AAers know as *pills* and the professionals as *medication*. Many (again probably most) AAers are deathly afraid of them. The fear may not be rational, but it is entirely understandable. AAers know, better than most professionals, how susceptible they are to any sort of habit-forming substance. Professionals know, better than most AAers, that medication in the early stages of treatment is usually essential. But they need to see more clearly the necessity for controlling, limiting, and above all ending the use of drugs as soon as possible.

AA and professionals need each other. Quite likely, they will never agree entirely: a melding of a necessarily amorphous fellowship with scientific disciplines might be too much to hope for, and perhaps not even a good thing if it were possible. But better understanding on both sides certainly is urgently required. As younger and generally better-informed alcoholics continue to swell the AA ranks and as more and more professionals and para-professionals enter the field, progress is possible and sometimes even visible. But far more empathy and far greater effort are needed for a better-directed assault upon the common enemy.

The foregoing was written by a successful AA member. It represents a point of view which is no longer unusual, although it is far from universal. It was produced by a man who knows, loves, and respects the fellowship, having come to it after having been helped by a psychiatrist.

Some hard things need to be said straight out.

The professional who does not knowledgeably and routinely refer to AA is not competent. The clinical psychology graduate student who spends five or six postgraduate years learning his trade, but never manages to attend a meeting, who thinks of a referral to AA, or who identifies an alcohol problem in a caseload containing 30 to 60 percent alcohol-associated disorders is something of a jackass, and so are his teachers. The AA person who takes pills away from a "pigeon" without knowing what's in them (heart medication, diabetes medication, anti-convulsant medication, etc.) is as dangerous as the physician who prescribes medication for alcohol-troubled people either without knowing that an alcohol problem exists or without having informed himself of the special dangers of using some specific medications with the addictive or chemically oriented individual.

Include nurses, psychiatric social workers, psychiatrists in the list. If they do not have an adequate understanding of AA, gained through personal, not second-hand, contact, they have failed to learn their professions thoroughly.

On the other hand, Alcoholics Anonymous members and the fellowship itself need to take some long, hard looks at their stances on a number of important matters. Since AA is an aggregation of individual people, it is often difficult to get a handle on official positions of the fellowship. Sometimes the official position is substantially different from that generated by the out-in-the-world members and groups. Further, it is not unusual to hear expositions of AA "policies" toward "alcoholics" and "alcoholism" which are expressed with great conviction and finality as group findings or beliefs, but which turn out to be the private opinions of the speaker, who then says that there is no official policy and that he is speaking only for himself. It is neither possible nor fair nor helpful to have it both ways.

As I have indicated in preceding chapters, most of society and even most AA members substantially underestimate the numbers of people who have alcohol troubles and overestimate the difficulties in helping. Difficulty in helping should not be used as a kind of retroactive diagnostic tool, as in, "If he's hard to help, he's an alcoholic," or conversely, "She quit so quickly—or so easily—that she obviously wasn't a *real* alcoholic."

Some counting and assessment problems are connected with AA. It is abundantly clear that no one person, agency or fellowship has all the answers. On sheer numbers alone this is evident, since AA does not even *reach* half or one tenth of the people troubled with alcohol *even once*, never mind help them. Because counting and evaluation of outcome is not one of AA's real interests, it is difficult to assess its effectiveness beyond a subjective conviction that it helps a lot of people.

The figure that was so popular (and inaccurate) for so long ("AA helps over 50 percent") clearly needs revision downward, not as a statement that AA is not helpful (for it would not be possible to find any group which has been of even equal help), but as a simple statement of reality. That downward revision has been taking place for several years; one first heard it privately and now more openly from some AA members.

It is quite possible—even probable—that fewer than half of the individuals who do get to AA for one meeting return for as many as five times in their lives. The argument that they are not ready doesn't wash: it is somebody's responsibility to help them to get ready, especially since we know we can do that with considerable success.

The argument that if people will follow the program they'll recover from their alcoholism only means that if it works, it works. Nobody can argue with that, certainly, but one can argue with the all-too-popular assumption that if somebody who is in trouble can't do what you want him to do, it's his fault, not yours. Many community mental health clinics do this when they "explain" a low hit rate or a failure of a client to return often enough to get help by saying, "His motivation was poor."

One who works with alcohol troubled people outside of AA is privileged eventually to know and admire many successful AA people and many people who have done just as well without it as well.

It is helpful in this regard that so many AA oriented people are going into treatment and outreach programs as helpers, supported by federal, state, or local tax dollars. In these settings, they are now meeting many people who have been turned off by AA, or who are unable to relate to it yet (one always hopes that people will go back to AA under new circumstances and catch on if they didn't before). This expansion into setting where AA failures become more visible than at AA meetings, which are selective in that the successful members are visible for a long time while the unsuccessful ones drop out and become invisible, will, I hope, assist the fellowship to keep looking for even better ways, with open minds.

Unfortunately, many people simply will not go to AA. To ask why is a legitimate question, which probably has no one answer, but asking it could lead to new attitudes, styles, and comprehensions.

One must be pained by the long adherence of some AAers to the "low bottom" theory and on the other hand delighted by an increased ability to set bottom higher. If the old folklore of "low bottom" had been found to be lacking, and it has, then wouldn't it now be useful to say,

"We made some errors in the past, let's try to reduce and shorten errors in the future"?

It is helpful to some people to be inculcated with the idea that they cannot take one drink because it will lead to more. It is truly unwise for an ATP to take one drink, but why not say exactly that, instead of "If you take one drink you won't be able to stop"? Another possibility is to say, "If you've been damfool enough to take one, for God's sake quit there. You can, you know, and I expect you to. You can no longer avoid the issue by moaning that you're lost and have to drink a lot because you're hopeless and took one drink. I do not urge you to take the one, but if you should, don't take two. And if you catch yourself at two, don't make it worse with three or a binge." Many people, even some long-term and chronic alcoholics in the old definitions, can sometimes drink a little here and there and then stop. But we also believe that sooner or later, usually sooner, they will probably get caught again, and then they won't stop on that occasion.

This is not to argue for taking the first drink. It is most preferable not to. This is an argument for being realistic; taking one drink cannot be permitted to be the reason for taking more.

AA people have an unfortunate tendency as a mass or aggregate to attack and drive away anyone who doesn't totally agree or who is just learning, although this trait, too, is happily diminishing. They do this especially to professionals, particularly to young ones, who then decide it isn't worth getting roughed up and bad-mouthed, so they stop dealing with alcohol troubled people. This happens despite the long history of professional admiration for Alcoholics Anonymous, and despite the fact that a co-founder was Dr. Bob, and that Dr. Silkworth was such a staunch and very early supporter. "Without its friends in medicine, Alcoholics Anonymous might never have been born." (p. 235, *Alcoholics Anonymous Comes of Age*)

To remember the hurts one has suffered at the hands

of untutored professionals, be they medical or otherwise, is natural. The only reasonable response possible is to tutor them, inform them, and draw them into the alcohol orbit, and then to urge them in turn to tutor AA people in the professional's useful set of skills and outlooks.

I very much dislike the duplicity that is "forced" out of some AA members and on members by the vehemence and conviction with which pronouncements about alcohol problems are often delivered. Such powerful group pressures tend to shut down innovative thinking about the issues, a circumstance we cannot afford until we have all the answers. Diversity of viewpoints is healthy, as long as it is thoughtful and leads to improvement. I am stunned by professionals who have serious disagreements with AA in private and say only laudatory things about it in public rather than have to defend their views against assault— not disagreement, but emotional assault. I am almost as disappointed by AA members who urge dissenters, in private, "What you are saying is so right, keep it up. I just wanted you to know but I don't dare say it in the meeting."

I cannot agree with sponsors calling their people "pigeons" or "babies". That is demeaning.

It is counterproductive for AAers, successful or not, to speak as if only AA can be helpful, with the implication that if you can't make it in AA that is necessarily the end of you.

An AA friend of mine has recently been troubled by an AA advertisement, "If you want to drink, that's your business. If you want to stop, that's ours." He wanted it in the book that alcohol trouble is everybody's business, because we all pay taxes and extra hospital and insurance bills, and risk our lives on roads shared by drinking drivers.

AA has to ask the same kind of questions that any other helping group or individual should ask: "Are we helping?" (Definitely and unequivocally yes, and in large numbers.) "In helping many, are we doing something that is hurting others? If so, how many and how badly?" (Definitely yes; in large numbers; and very badly.)

AA has a strong and widespread influence for both good and ill. People must realize that alcohol-impaired people may need assistance from many different sources and points of view. Some individuals can arrest their problems *only* in some way other than AA. Some can do it only with AA conjunction with something else, and some with AA only.

My restiveness with AA is vastly less than with members of my own profession and other related professions, but it is necessary, as I've indicated, to call a spade a spade with all who have a stake in improving the lot of our large alcohol troubled population. AA is changing with the times quite rapidly; its overall scope cannot be matched. It is my belief that it will continue to do well and even to improve its effectiveness.

In closing this chapter, I urge everyone interested in, or affected by, alcohol troubles to relate to Alcoholics Anonymous. If it is to assist the helper, or the spouse, or the primary person, or the student, or whoever you are, I've sent you to the right people. The chances are excellent that you will find yourself among extremely warm, caring and committed people.

If it doesn't help, try something or someone else. Perhaps you will discover AA's value in another time or place, as many have done before you.

But keep trying.

8
Taking Action, or Digging Out of Trouble

The great thing is to prevent his doing anything. As long as he does not convert it into action, it does not matter how much he thinks about this new repentance. . . . Let him do anything but act. No amount of piety in his imagination . . . will harm us if we can keep it out of his will. As one of the humans has said, active habits are strengthened by repetition but passive ones are weakened. The more often he feels without acting, the less he will ever be able to act, and, in the long run, the less he will be able to feel.

A demon to his apprentice, on capturing souls, from
The Screwtape Letters, C. S. Lewis

You have already taken some action—you have begun to inform yourself. If I have done my job, the information and attitudes to which you have been exposed are accurate, realistic, and practical. I have tried to establish a base from which to work. I have also presented a number of techniques and modes of viewing the problem that can be used as tools for getting out of trouble. Just one such example was the discussion of ways to overcome the social pressures to drink in Chapter 5.

In other words, much of the material presented earlier relates logically to the present chapter.

Earlier chapters have debunked some myths and have suggested useful and nonuseful ways of determining when alcohol troubles exist. You know that tackling the problems inherent in alcohol usage is done much better sooner than later, but that in any event alcohol troubles are a distinctly reparable disorder.

You have gathered that I believe you need more, much more, than the sheer information provided here or elsewhere. To do anything useful you must also develop an entire new set of attitudes and feelings about alcohol troubles and about people who have them—and that includes feelings toward yourself if you have begun to run afoul of booze.

The major barrier between you and helpful information, or between you and the attitude you'll need to develop, may well be a modest difficulty in accepting a change in yourself. We in alcohol work have grown used to informing people in the best ways we can think of, only to find a resistance to change.

Against this background I introduce the word *neurotic* into our conversation. This word is borrowed from the mental health disciplines and has many unpleasant connotations, mostly because people don't understand what it means. It means, simply, "inflexible and stupid." One knows he is dealing with neurotic behavior when someone who is not dumb in most life areas is dumb in one or two, and we know that such a person is inflexible if he or she keeps *repeating* a particular set of mistakes *as if* he or she were really stupid. Each of us is neurotically inflexible and stupid about some areas—frequent hot spots in this regard are money, relationships to authority, affection and sex, and the handling of anger.

When confronted with certain situations, we all dance our own little neurotic, repetitive, ritualistic dances. Another major hot spot is the area of booze, not only in the person who actually has the problem but often in the person who wants to help. The tendency toward inflexibility and repetitive use of techniques or systems that may not work well or could work much better is very strong indeed in the human beast. Some people in alcohol work have a particularly powerful tendency to attempt progress by applying more energy and money to ways of doing things that have never proved optimal. It's like the patient whose medication is not working, so he insists that his physician give him more of it.

We have experienced much positive change in the last few years. We now need an ability to experiment with additional possibilities and new modes of thought and to sharpen some of our old ones.

Among the priorities which I have touched on earlier is to change our outlook from "Alcoholics are really tough to change" to *"Alcohol-impaired people have good outcomes far oftener than we have allowed ourselves to believe."* Some still hold, in spite of abundant evidence to the contrary, that alcohol problems are intransigent and improve only as a result of miracles. That is a neurotic (inflexible and stupid) position and calls for alterations in styles and perceptions. If *all* a helper sees are losers or slow winners in his work, then he must be doing something wrong.

The physician or psychologist or social worker who never succeeds when working with alcohol troubled people is obviously repeating the same unhelpful behavior, attitude and information in client after client. Such people would be better off not working with the problem, but in fact we do not have that luxury—they're working with it anyway without knowing it. It is *not possible* to work alertly and skillfully in this area and not have a substantial hit rate; in addition, we do better as we continue to learn.

The wife who applies the same formula to her problem husband year after year would do better to stop applying larger and larger doses of what isn't helping, whether it's excess love and understanding or kicking him out of the house every once in a while. If it doesn't work, she should find another way.

I could, but won't, include a long discussion on "Stumbling Blocks in the Way of Progress: The Inability of Agents and Agencies of Change to Permit Change." Much of that difficulty revolves around man's sense of security in acting, and feeling, in the old familiar way.

I hope this book will reach several kinds of readers, in no particular order of importance:

- Helpers, whether "professionals" or others.
- Primary, or alcohol troubled, persons, at whatever level of damage.
- Families, employers, friends, and colleagues of ATPs.
- College and high-school students, who constitute a large, affected, eager-to-learn group.
- Alcohol program policy-makers (local, state, and federal).
- Professional educators, who are going to prove crucial in educational efforts.

People in these categories may have somewhat different group goals, but they do have one thing in common: because of the huge numbers of people in trouble with alcohol, almost anyone may be, or could be, a primary person as well as a high-school student, or a helping professional whose daughter or wife is high-risk or a primary person, and so on.

In this chapter I must grapple with everyone's quite natural desire for a cookbook. If Charlie does *A*, then what do I as a helper do? What is step *B*? It seems that there must be an orderly sequence of *A*, *B*, *C*, and *D*. In helping alcohol troubled people, however, many variables affect the outcome—the skills of the therapist, the reliability of his or her intuition, the resources available, the problem and personality of the patient, and so on.

So I will not use a cookbook approach, and I strongly suggest that you overcome the desire for one. We need instead to rely on a mixture of principles and practical techniques, emphasizing that throughout our work we must remain receptive and keep learning. If you are the primary person in trouble, you've made mistakes and are in a position to learn from them. If you are a helper, even a long-time and skillful one, you too have made plenty of mistakes. If you're a beginning helper, remember that you learn through amassing wins and losses and by evaluating them nonneurotically. Then next time you can take a little bit of what *worked* last time, if it fits the new situation. This, of course, is called experience. (See also Sir William Osler's quote at the beginning of Chapter 4.)

The rest of the chapter is devoted to practical principles and techniques for use in digging out of trouble.

Recognizing the Existence of Choice

At some point, hopefully, you will learn that the task is *either to reestablish the option for choice or to help the alcohol-impaired person realize that choice remains*, even if it may not seem that way at the moment. Contrary to popular opinion, very few people truly have lost the ability to choose whether to drink or not. In my observation, those few who have actually lost the capacity to choose are in serious physiological trouble, often suffering addiction and its components—increased tolerance and withdrawal symptoms. Yet even these people have not all lost the ability to exercise choice.

Many people in alcohol trouble believe they have lost the power of choice partly because they are repeatedly told that they have. Additionally—and many of us have failed to notice this fact—people in alcohol trouble want to stop *and also want not to stop*. Those who claim that all power of choice is lost tend to deal with one or the other, when it is much more helpful to recognize that *both* are true.

Much of the world functions on the basis of the "either/ or error," the assumption that either one thing is true *or* its opposite is true. Johnny is honest or dishonest, according to the either/or error, even if experience shows that he is dishonest sometimes, perhaps when he is afraid of his father, and honest at other times, perhaps when he is taking a test or playing a card game. This horse is either a good horse or a bad horse, according to the either/or error, even if it would be more useful to say he pulls well but runs abominably, or he is vicious when you're afoot in his stall, but he can win the Belmont Stakes.

When people go awry there are very often several interlocking causes, not just one. To believe that a teen-ager with acne has merely neglected to wash her face (which can be one cause) is to ignore the effect of diet and hormonal changes. High blood pressure can be due to one causal factor such as kidney damage or can be related to diet, anger, stress, *and/or* a myriad of other factors or any combination thereof.

The people around the primary person get discouraged when they focus only on the fact that "He said he wanted to quit," but so does the primary person himself, who continuously tells himself the same thing. All concerned would do much better to accept that wanting to stop drinking is a genuine desire but is not the whole story. Recall that alcohol dissolves immediate anxiety and stress very quickly. It is therefore only natural and to be expected (and accepted) that there should be a powerful urge to use it. It is not appropriate to regard the alcohol-involved person as weak or dishonest just because *both* you and he failed to notice the simultaneous existence of two competing desires.

It is not profitable to act as if the thought in the foreground is the only motivation—always recall that the competing, opposite urge lurks in the shadows and that that knowledge can be utilized to great profit.

If we resist the either/or error, we have a distinct new weapon at hand. By manipulating either the environment or the tension we can in fact make one side predominate while remaining alert to the other, competing side of the coin, which is always there, should no longer surprise us, and can be used positively if we can be creative after we register its existence.

Always—except in the *severe* and *occasional* physiological instance mentioned earlier—the individual has considerable choice. If he does not know that he does, it is up to someone to point out the fact and to tell him that what happens to each person is largely a function of his choice.

Let me use an example: A squash court is a good-sized room painted all white except for a red line here and there. The ball can be played off each surface except the ceiling, and because of this fact the small door by which one enters is designed to permit a ball to bounce true off it. The cracks around the door are very small because it fits well, and the handle is engineered to fold in and thus present a flat surface.

If you knew nothing about this arrangement and were brought into it blindfolded (or better yet, markedly inebriated) you would probably not see for a time that there was a door, especially if you were scared or confused or not functioning well in general. Imagine that the alcohol-impaired person is in a situation comparable to a squash court with several well-disguised doors that we know about but he doesn't. As he gains information about these means of escape he regains choice of action.

The *awareness of choice* is a useful tool for digging out of alcohol troubles. That we cannot in most life situations actually give up choice, even though we may become unaware for a time that we actually retain it, is an existential fact, and so we remain responsible, whether we like it or not, for a great amount of what happens to us. The alcohol-involved person, when he is beginning to regain his freedom of action, is hesitant to face the total loss of his "friendly" chemical forever, and it is often helpful to him, in approaching sobriety, to shoot for the attainment of alternatives (which are not broadly available while drinking) rather than total, forever abstinence. It is helpful and quite honest to emphasize that more alternatives are available to such a person by cutting back or giving up on alcohol. To be honest when taking this tack, one must *truly* want to restore freedom of choice with regard to the drink or not-drink issue. It is not necessary early in the game, but generally not a bit harmful, to point out to the sufferer that you genuinely wish to help him regain freedom of choice and that you believe when he has it back he will choose not to drink because by then he will feel good in lots of ways, and being proud of himself will be one of them.

Some helpers maintain that the individual has nothing to say about his drinking—that he has lost the power not to drink—but, peculiarly, that he retains his choice of whether to take his Antabuse, attend AA seven nights a week, or show up for his doctor's appointment. This is selective and inconsistent; it is better to clarify to the person that he indeed has power and responsibility.

In almost every instance, then, the choice and therefore the responsibility lies ultimately with the drinker, although others can and do help or hinder. That he or she may have to learn these facts does not alter the basic truth that choice always *exists*.

The knowledge that one possesses the choice whether to drink or not can only be encouraging, since it presents an immediate degree of freedom to begin quick constructive action.

Above and before everything else, you must continually recall that *you are the agent and instrument of change.* Helper or primary person, if you keep making the same kinds of mistakes and cannot seem to develop a fairly broad helping attitude, check to see if you are being inflexible and stupid. Do *not* do more of what has not helped, whether you are yourself in alcohol trouble or are a helper.

You should develop the habit of *pursuing therapeutic advantage* wherever you find it. Aim for targets of opportunity—be creative enough to make them if they don't occur spontaneously. If he won't go to AA, *you* go, especially if he's been resisting going alone. You'll learn something, make friends who might have some ideas, and maybe he'll feel so left out he'll go, or more likely, he'll get so suspicious about what you're saying there that he'll go to make sure they hear his side of it. And if that doesn't work, try something else, but for heaven's sake don't do the same old thing for eight years if it doesn't work.

Sticking to the Issue

Be ruthless with yourself about *going in a straight line;* if your goal is to get rid of alcohol troubles, go after it. Staying on the trail of the problem is a skill that has to be developed, and some people have terrible difficulties learning how. One may have to be impolite or accept being disliked—it's not only acceptable but often necessary to interrupt a complicated, twisting story designed to demonstrate how impossible it is to deal with the issue right now. A lot of mental health workers are bad at going in a straight line, for two reasons. First, they secretly believe that something else is really more important than the alcohol problem and they go after that instead. Second, there are many Jews in mental health professions, and since their subculture doesn't have an alcohol problem, they sometimes have trouble believing and understanding, in their bones and corpuscles. Some spouses have troubles sticking to the trail. AA old-timers are great in this department—they're like wise old hounds who don't pay any attention to the fox's tricks. They know just about what he'll do, and they stick to the issue.

A lot of old evasions seem shiny bright and new to the ATP first using them. There's the woman who's going to quit after the holidays—she doesn't want to ruin her family's good times. The children will be returning for Thanksgiving and she doesn't want to be a wet blanket. (They'd all be tickled silly, of course.) There's the executive who will take a shot at it after the quarterly reports are in. He says

he needs his sleep and can't afford to start shaking now
because he needs his wits about him. Or, "There's a long
weekend coming up at the end of the month; I'll do it then.
My wife and I will get away to the Cape, and I'll quit under
less pressured circumstances."

It is helpful in the task of going in a straight line, of
staying fixed on the alcohol situation, to learn to *think by
exception*. Ask yourself: "Are there exceptions to this statement he is laying before me as if it were a Holy Rule or an
unassailable Reason for Drinking?" If his reason is physical
pain, ask yourself: "Has anyone ever suffered pain before
without turning to alcohol to kill it?" If so, there is an exception to the rule that is being offered as a reason for this
individual to drink. Similarly, ask yourself whether others
have ever lost a beloved mother—or lost a promotion, or
won the sweepstakes, or flunked out of college, or had a
shabby upbringing—without turning to booze. If you can
answer yes when you look for an exception, you will no
longer need to be confused by the irrelevancies that initially
sound so important.

For reasons largely based on faulty definitions of alcohol problems ("I can't be an alcoholic because . . ."), one
of the most familiar dodges is "There's no reason for me to
stop because I can stop anytime." Illogically, the person is
saying "I won't stop because I can."

> The logical response from the helper is: "I never said
> you couldn't stop. In fact, I believe you can or I wouldn't
> be spending my time with you. You seem to be using 'I
> can stop' to tell me you're not an alcoholic, but I've never
> called you one. All I'm concerned about is that you have
> problems because you drink, and *that's* why you should
> stop. I *didn't* ask you to stop because I think you can't
> stop. A lot of people are exceptions to your 'rule'—they
> stopped simply because they *could* and it was hurting
> them not to."

I know a young therapist who was interested in alcohol

problems and their relationship to family unit difficulties and mental health problems. He took on a family in which the wife had a significant alcohol problem. In my terms, she was on the borderline between moderate and severe in degree. She was attractive, fastidiously groomed and dressed, very bright, and in no way looked or talked like a drunk.

She first saw the therapist at the beginning of a sober stretch, but soon she began explaining how difficult her husband was. She began to drink. He was brought in, as he should have been, but probably in this case he was brought in for the wrong reason—to see if he was difficult enough to be *causing her to drink*. (The position should have been: "We'll see him after you've stopped drinking for two or three days. You drink because you choose to. Many women have difficult husbands but don't get in trouble with the bottle. So if we see that your husband is a difficult person that will not prove to be very relevant to the issue before us today—the fact that you're drinking again.")

The therapist showed further difficulty going in a straight line when the husband *did* prove difficult and attempts were made to change the husband's behavior—not as a reward to the woman for not drinking but as a *means* to get her to stop.

At this point the trust in the helper-helpee relationship began to erode, and time was spent on that. And so forth. Not a straight line.

At some point in this case the issue might have been put back in focus without offending anyone or driving anyone away by using the simile of a lumberjack who is about to fell a large tree (the woman's emotional and family problems) but who can't get near enough to swing his axe because vines and underbrush (alcohol usage) are tripping him up, snagging his axe, shortening his swing, and generally confusing him. "So let's get the underbrush out of the way. We can do that quickly and then we won't have to mess with it. In a lot of cases we find that when alcohol is no longer an issue the other problems evaporate. But if the other problems remain *after* alcohol is no longer a factor, at least we'll be able to see the size and shape of them and work on them efficiently, which we simply cannot do while you're drinking."

This is a true statement; it helps the patient save face (you have recognized that there may be another problem); and you have promised a reward *in addition to* getting out of the alcohol troubles of which she is aware. You say you'll pay her off for doing well with alcohol, so you *stay on the issue!*

To go in a straight line—to stay fastened on the central issue of alcohol—feels rude and impolite to some helpers. It isn't. A helper needs to develop a willingness to be no-nonsense at times, and it is rude only to give less than your best. It appears extraordinary to beginning helpers in alcohol troubles that most helpees are *not* offended by straight talk. Sometimes, to be sure, they are, but fear of offending cannot be permitted to interfere with the core issue, either.

If a man believes he is in alcohol trouble because his wife is impossible, for example, it is acceptable to suggest in the interest of clarity that he has the following alternatives:

1. Run away, change his name, and disappear from his wife forever, rather than destroy himself with booze.
2. Divorce or separate from her.
3. Mount a counterattack, in which case he cannot possibly win if he is in a confused, alcohol troubled position. He will need his wits about him because she's been at this a long time and is very good at it.
4. Find a very high bridge or another means of ending it all. This way out of drinking has the advantages of being less damaging to family finances and one's psyche, and usually of being less demoralizing and physically painful than using alcohol to die by inches. It carries the disadvantages of letting his wife have the last word and thus winning the contest, and of putting the man

in the shameful position of having said, "I'll kill myself rather than give up my bottle or deal with my wife in some coping fashion."

That is what I mean by going in a straight line. People drink because they have learned to and not because they have no choice; thinking by exception will demonstrate that.

You may find it useful to examine whether you are ashamed, either for the drinker or for yourself if you are the drinker. If your embarrassment for the other person hinders you from jumping in and calling a spade a spade, the problem of course is that you think what the person is doing is weak or immoral, and if you yourself were in need of that kind of help you'd be ashamed. If that is the case, you need to work on your attitudes toward alcohol-impaired people; who gave you the right to be ashamed for *them*?

Not long ago I was working with a sharp and relatively courageous graduate student who ordinarily was willing to try new things. She somehow managed, however, for week after week not to visit and begin to deal with the alcohol troubled parent of a grown client, despite the fact that the parent's problem, bad enough in its own right, was foiling the therapeutic efforts with the offspring. It finally came down to the nitty-gritty—the student was too ashamed for the parent to be able to get into the alcohol with him. She wondered how she would start, and how she could handle the situation smoothly without upsetting him. What she didn't know is that if she had had her own attitudes squared away it would be pretty hard to say the "wrong" thing. She might, it is true, pull a minor goof, but it probably wouldn't be very important, because the intent and attitude would be helpful, and that generally carries the day.

Finally the student got to the house but in her shame for the man was unable to broach the subject. Another student made a helpful suggestion, "If you noticed a sore or a cut on him when you went to the house, and it looked as if it weren't healing, you'd mention it, wouldn't you?" He shouldn't have to be sick and miserable just because we are "sure" he'd be offended. If we think he's doing a "bad" thing because we ourselves would feel guilt-ridden if we were doing it, that's *our* problem.

Finally I went out with the graduate student and the man was easily engageable—contact was made and the subject discussed without difficulty.

Here, then, was a bit of neuroticism on our parts, and a little unconscious dishonesty too. We are the people who say one shouldn't be ashamed of having problems and getting help with them, yet here was a helper who clearly felt shame and didn't even know it.

I'm reminded of the time we were starting a mental health clinic on a university campus, and the staff and trainees, almost none of whom had ever worked in such a place, spent hour after unproductive hour worrying about how to sneak clients into the building unobserved and not let them see one another—in a waiting room for example—once in.

That whole train of thought—shame for others because in the minds of the therapists there would be shame in them—should have unraveled when one of the therapists reported that she had been shopping that week in the supermarket and one of her clients had called her from across the store and asked when her next appointment was.

There is no inherent shame in having alcohol troubles—the shame, very simply, is in not doing something about them.

Being Consistent and Honest

I have mentioned the base of information and attitude that must be developed. Another critical base is the principle of honesty, of consistency, of saying only what you believe, and of dredging through your head, over and over and always, to determine when you have changed your view, or to ferret out ways in which you are not being straight.

Tom was admitted to a general hospital with alcoholic cirrhosis. His judgment and ability to think were temporarily damaged and his body was in very serious trouble. About two months after admission he was transferred to the alcohol unit.

He was unhappy to be labeled an alcoholic (which we would not now do to him). He came from a small town, and it had been his habit to go each day to a particular bar on one of the two main streets. Since he was too fouled up to hold a job, his wife was working and Tom was left in charge of their youngest child, a five-year-old boy. Every day he left the child to fend for himself on the steps and sidewalk outside the bar while he himself drank for five or six hours.

The policy on the alcohol unit was to involve the spouses in treatment and also to require the individual to go to Alcoholics Anonymous, at least on a trial basis. Tom was reluctant to attend AA, saying, "I can do it myself," and was obviously ashamed to be thus identified. His wife, interestingly enough, didn't want him to go to AA because then "Everybody will know Tom's an alcoholic."

Between the two of them—the severely alcohol-impaired man and the wife who needed help in helping him— they resisted his going to AA for several weeks. It was, in fact, the first time they'd pulled together in some months. The wife's reason was clearly based on something other than common sense, although she was certainly a bright person. She was ashamed and frightened of her family's situation and much preferred to deny it was happening— even when denial made poor sense. Everyone in the town knew Tom was in alcohol trouble—he was unemployed, often intoxicated, his wife had gone back to work, and finally he had landed in the hospital. If they had somehow missed the point, he had placed his kid like a neon sign in front of the bar, day after day.

Each of these individuals was burdened with counterproductive, useless shame. The wife, for a time, had difficulty being straight, speaking about wanting Tom to be out of trouble and at the same time sabotaging efforts to help.

Central to being honest is noting whether or not your *behavior* is consistent with your words or thoughts. One has to question the honesty of a person who claims to love animals but kicks the dog or starves the cat. Sometimes the best way to discover a dishonesty in oneself or others is to check for a substantial disparity between word and deed. When in doubt believe the deed.

The exercise would help the professional therapist who says there is no shame in coming for professional help but is too embarrassed to raise "shameful" issues or takes great pains to hide clients, or doesn't know whether it's all right to speak to them on the street. Readers outside these professions may doubt the existence of such humanness—it is much with us, believe me.

I do not often see duplicitous psychotherapists or alcohol helpers become much less duplicitous, because they tend to be too self-protective and it costs a lot to note one's own dishonesty. Since we are all inconsistent or dishonest at times, no matter how we try, it is doubly important that helpers be persons who value, and can take the rigors of, criticism of themselves and their duplicity. It is an article of faith for me that one simply cannot be an optimal, or even a reasonably good, helper if not fastidious in this regard.

It is acceptable to make mistakes in this area but not to persist in them, and certainly not to blind oneself to them. Beginning helpers continuously ask how to approach this subject or that with a helpee. Spouses, colleagues, friends, children all sometimes suffer from this inability to speak the truth. If your attitude is helpful, just say what's on your mind. It will almost always work out fine. If your pose is to be helpful but something else is more important—such as being smarter, or more powerful, or appearing better ad-

justed than the helpee, or doing your job better than your
co-worker—you may fail when broaching a touchy subject;
because you'll foul it up with an intonation, a hesitation,
or a facial expression.

It is easy to be duplicitous in many areas in alcohol
work:

Forcing a person into admitting he is "an alcoholic"
when he is not ready often serves the purpose of making
the so-called helper comfortable, but may quickly drive the
potential helpee away. In my opinion that kind of thing is
dishonest, since it is our announced task only to help the
person, and it is abundantly clear that many are helped
without being forced into the role of a groveling supplicant.

I once spoke at a general medical hospital that had just
received a large federal alcohol grant and had hired a hard-
lining recovering ATP as a counselor. He missed my talk,
in which I suggested that helpers consider not forcing this
admission, especially in the early phases of engagement,
since to do so is to lose an extremely high proportion of
prospective helpees.

A few days later a friend who also worked at the hospital reported hearing the hard-liner badgering, brow-beat-
ing, and generally demeaning a drunk to try to get him to
admit he needed help, that anybody could see he was an
alcoholic and he'd better face it (while intoxicated, yet!)
and so forth. They lost the guy, of course.

I know a young man who almost never fails to get ATPs
back for further dealings; he is far less experienced (in
years) than the hard-lining harasser, but light years ahead
in effectiveness. This guy wants to be of use, not just win
in a temporary power struggle.

Another popular and duplicitous game is the one I call
"*I gotcha*" or "*I gotcha, you liar.*" I recall the helper who
became alerted to the possibility of alcohol troubles in a
female client and asked her about drinking. The question
must have been asked in a way that said "I'm ready to

pounce if you say yes," because the helpee denied ever
drinking. A year or so later she smelled of alcohol, and then
the pounce came.

It is far better to feel and communicate "I just want
to be of use, not to catch you." In the foregoing instance the
helper could have said very openly that often in situations
like this one alcohol plays a part, that the helper sees sug-
gestive signs of it, that other problems evaporate with surprising speed when alcohol intake is reduced, and that it
therefore makes sense to talk about the alcohol component
together. If I were pretty sure, I think I wouldn't even ask
but would simply assume we would talk about it, relying
on the assumption to obviate the need for defensive lying
and denial.

It's easy to be straight when you have no "reason" not
to be, but you must be honest even when it's difficult, not
just when there's no discomfort or doubt. Principles are
especially useful when there is a reason for them.

Sometimes a helper can best be straight simply by an-
nouncing his intention. "What I think we should do is get
you off booze for a couple of weeks to see if you'll do better.
I know that if I ask you to do that it may seem too big a
task right now, so I'm going to shoot for a time you can
deliver. How about a couple of days? You understand that
after that time I'll finagle for another agreement. Maybe
at the end of two weeks we'll agree, or I'll insist, that you
should quit for longer, but we can work on that in a couple
of weeks when you're feeling less scared." And so forth.

I won't say "Maybe at the end of two weeks" and so on
if there isn't any maybe about it. If I am sure that he is
going to have to stop I'll say that—to do otherwise is to be
untrustworthy. (Besides, I have a lousy memory and if I
lied I'd always tell a second, different lie and be found
out.) Sometimes a helper does say one thing at one time
and a different thing later, but the change should always be
based on a revised set of perceptions. If the patient questions such a changed message, it is easy and truthful, if

one has been scrupulous, to indicate that you're pretty sure he's right, but if you said something different at an earlier time it was because that's what you believed at the time and it now appears that the earlier statement was in error.

I have learned that whenever a helper speaks of "confronting," he refers to a combination of "I gotcha, you liar" and a beating down argument foisted by the helper on the helpee. *Confrontation* is one of those words with vast emotional meaning—we rarely, if ever, make progress in a confrontation atmosphere.

Confronting is a duplicitous game in which the confronter is actually engaged not in helping, but in satisfying his own power needs. The confronter mounts an assault, and, having put himself in a position to lose face if he doesn't win, quite naturally convinces himself that he *must* win in order to convince the helpee, and thus "help" him by beating him.

Sometimes helpees need to win a little bit to make progress. I am constitutionally unable to let even five-year-olds beat me at Ping-Pong—they can beat me only when they're good enough to beat me. In the meantime I don't have to get my kicks out of playing competitively with them or with confused, easily beatable alcohol-impaired people. On the other hand, most people who are five-year-olds or are alcohol troubled are rewarding to be with, but not in the context of power struggles.

If you're always first with the right answer, neither five-year-olds nor alcohol-damaged people will grow or will be willing to spend time with you. And the name of the game is growth in their functioning and coping abilities.

Another ready opportunity to be duplicitous in alcohol work was mentioned earlier, and that is in the area of calling a spade a spade. Generally it is best to label the problem *if you care* what is happening to the person in alcohol difficulties and/or if it is your job. (The two may coincide or at least overlap.) Someone has to be the first to say it, and if you are concerned enough to open the subject this year and

you don't hit, perhaps someone else will do it next year.
Thus, the individual has an opportunity to be informed of
his problem or perhaps to become convinced that it's getting
visible to other people and therefore requires attention.

If you don't care enough about the individual to take
the possible flak, don't call it and don't feel guilty. You are
not required to save the world at any cost to yourself. I
have, for example, worked with a psychiatrist with a moderate to severe alcohol problem, but I don't care enough to
take the static that would be forthcoming if I discussed it,
and I don't feel a second's guilt.

If you yourself have a problem, or if somebody has said
you do but you can't yet believe, think a little more—it
wasn't all that easy for your friend to mention the possibility to you, and you can be sure it wasn't done idly.

It is *not* straight to *pretend* you care and then not run
the risk of calling the shot. It is also not straight to be
brutally frank, as some people are in these situations. If
you intend to communicate helpfully you must transmit the
message in such a way that it has a chance to be received.
Being brutal by "letting it all hang out" activates so much
hurt and defensiveness that you have not communicated,
only hurt. If you said you wanted to communicate and instead were only brutal, you were not acting honestly.

Knowing the Person You are Helping

In attempting to communicate, you will do better if
you know who you're dealing with. If you are being helped,
assist your helper to know you as well as possible.

*Get to know the person you are helping and learn to
make deals* that will meet your goals of alcohol repair, and
his or her goals of getting out of trouble, in ways comfortable
to his personality style.

It is clear, for example, that some ATPs are so depressed or confused that they basically want to die but
haven't the courage, the energy, or the religion for the task.

So they drink themselves slowly, painfully, and untidily to their deaths without recognizing or accepting responsibility for their action. Do not tell such a person it will kill him—that only ensures his continued imbibing (unless you want to use the ultimate dirty trick and tell him you've caught him, a good Catholic, trying to fool God—but better announce that one or you're getting crooked).

It is crucial to take the trouble to find the appropriate wavelength for each person. With a bright, intellectual person you can make certain assumptions that would be of little help in some tough, macho males. It was once of use to me and to a person with whom I was working to discover that she was second in her class, twenty years earlier, in a top-notch private college. Nobody does that on sheer intellect; they also need a competitive, grinding will to be high in the standings, which in turn strongly suggests that success in the area of intellectual prowess may be something for which the individual will work hard. Such a strong drive sustained her at one time for four long years and can sustain her again. She could not stop drinking for her children, her husband, her pride in overcoming tough circumstances, her terrible depression, or her mixed-up emotions. None of that had worked, and we know enough not to repeat an unproductive formula. I had to appeal to this person's brain and her need to be an intellectual achiever. As she began to make progress, I would say, "That was a very clever way to handle it, Mary. I have to give you an A plus for this week's work."

The machismo-driven blue collar worker who has beaten his wife repeatedly, breaking her ribs and forcing her to move out time and again because of his drinking is told flat out that the little bottle is bigger and tougher than he is. "I'm going to bet you're not man enough to live a week without it." The wager, a pack of cigarettes (what else?), is sealed with a manly handshake. He can't wait to come back next week to rub it in and collect. He is also angered and eager to show you (that smart aleck bastard) who can do what. After a successful week he comes in, blows off

steam and collects. Then you point out that he's making a
pretty big deal out of going a mere week without booze—
something that frail little old ladies have been known to do.
How about a carton bet on a month from today? "I don't
mind losing a pack to you, since I have a pretty good chance
at the carton. I'll see you once a week until then, and you
can bring me the carton as soon as you knuckle under to the
bottle. No, I'm not calling you an alcoholic; I'm just trying
to find out how much of a weakling you are. Maybe I'm
wrong—you did a tough thing this week—so far. And if
making these bets gets you to stop drinking, which is what
I'm up to, then you'll feel good about yourself." And you get
him to shake on it.

If a person is frightened of withdrawal, that's easy
enough to understand. I would be too, and it's my job to comprehend, support, and reduce the fear in realistic ways. The
deal you make is a promise to provide support and expert
help in exchange for a good try by the frightened person.

The common thread in these examples is that you pitch
in to do everything you reasonably can to get them through
to the other side, where they will again know the choice is
theirs. It will not do to get off the alcohol track as you go;
you always have to go in a straight line.

Recognizing and Rewarding All Successes

I have mentioned the general topic of *success* in alcohol
work. The rules are to *count all successes to reward partial
success generously,* and to *help the individual reward himself for success.*

The earlier the identification of the problem, the easier
it is to achieve and reward success, of course. It is important,
however, to concentrate on success at any level of alcohol
involvement, whether you are helping another person or
helping yourself.

I have referred to the nonusefulness of the view that if
a person overcomes alcohol troubles quickly and well he

"never had a real problem." I have emphasized the importance of calling alcohol-induced troubles exactly what they are rather than continuing to focus on the pessimistic aspects of the problem and labeling the whole mess a strange and unchanging disease called alcoholism. Further, it is inaccurate and destructive to insist that only helpers who were once ATPs have any answers because they are the only ones who can deal with cases of "alcoholism."

Most ATPs, by being told about the problems in a manner which permits them to hear, become quickly aware that they can help themselves, or can reach for help, and can subsequently eliminate their alcohol-generated troubles. This, I emphasize, occurs most frequently in the minimal and moderate categories of damage—a major reason for stressing wide education.

While it is manifestly true that we need knowledgeable people in the field, we can no longer permit the existence of a sarcastic, elitist cadre of "experts" who denigrate the efforts of everyone but themselves—particularly since their own energies are almost always heavily and narrowly packed into "late-stage alcoholics." This group is the major locus of the "exclusivity" propaganda that prevents earlier engagement of alcohol problems, turns off beginners in the helper ranks, and drives away the young people and nontraditionalists who want to help.

By adhering primarily to the exclusivists' views, we militate against counting all successes, and success breeds enthusiasm, money, a swelling of the ranks—and further success.

Some helpers have great difficulty rewarding *partial* success, yet doing so is vital in this work. I recall a man who was forty-eight years old and had been hospitalized forty-eight times for alcohol or alcohol-related problems like pneumonia, broken bones, TB, malnutrition—the classic hardcore case with a severe degree of damage. He had not had one voluntary day without alcohol since he was nineteen, except during hospitalizations and their accompanying relief from life stress he didn't drink, and during the war while on cruise in the navy he couldn't drink.

As a direct result of being in an alcohol treatment program he went dry for four tortured but pride-generating days on his own, out on the street. He then drank, came back into the program for ten days, went out and stayed dry for a week. In view of his history, that was a major accomplishment, and he had tried so hard you could cry. He was shot down by an old-time hard-liner, who felt driven to beat him over the head with the failure, rather than the success, of his efforts.

He made it anyway, after the hard-liner was eliminated from the scene.

The questions of success and partial success are intimately woven into the question of payoff and reward. Obviously major rewards are associated with digging oneself out of alcohol troubles; these rewards include relief from depression, confusion, family and job problems, physical pain, remorse and guilt, and so forth. The payoffs tend to increase considerably and often strikingly in a matter of weeks and months and are clearly our final goal.

In the meantime it is human nature to need a *quick* payoff, and the most widely available, quickest payoff is the self-administered one. A lot of people either never had the knack of self-reward or somehow lost it. That characteristic lack is certainly not confined to ATPs, but they are definitely not good at self-reward either.

It may seem to be a digression, but let's look at this area. If you're a primary person, or if you are trying to work with one, examine your functioning in school situations. Many students worry inordinately about grades and tests. In anticipation they convince themselves that they cannot pass an upcoming test. If you try to alleviate their anxiety, they hold onto it doggedly. It is as though working themselves up into a fear state is a security blanket. They are a little superstitious that if they don't worry they will fail, and they are trying to generate the optimal amount of concern; if properly scared they'll study, cram, and function under semiemergency conditions, which is how they've learned to do the best job.

It is instructive to watch and listen to these same people after they've passed the exam. They do not reward themselves but seem to go out of their way to refuse to admit they did an adequate job. They figured the teacher's quirks and studied what they knew he'd ask. Or they just got lucky and happened to know the answers to the particular questions on the test. Or they just happened to come out OK on the scaling of the class results. The course was too easy. The teacher was easily conned.

The ruling principle, the rubric under which they order their lives, is "Anything I can do isn't really worth doing." The inaccessible woman who would surely never even look at him develops serious flaws when she surprisingly accepts a date. "If she'll go out with me there's something seriously wrong with her."

If the ATP is of this persuasion, and a lot of them are, any reduction or cessation of drinking is turned into a non-accomplishment by a stratagem like one of these:

1. Oh, woe is me. I spent all these years screwing myself up. I should have done this long ago. Look at what I've done to myself.
2. I never could have done it by myself. I had to have help.
3. Oh, yeah. Well, I got by the weekend only because my boss visited us at the summer cottage, and I couldn't drink when he was there.
4. Sure I stopped for a couple of weeks, but I've done that before. It won't last.
5. I'm scared to death. When something goes OK for a while something terrible always happens later.

   And so forth.

It is as important to notice and emphasize success, even partial success, as it is to pursue the alcohol problem in a straight line without being led astray. Avoidances 1 through 5 were probably activated by an awareness that things had gone fairly well, or even terrifically well. Perhaps someone forced an "admission" out of the ATP. He probably did not speak of his success first, although failures are always mentioned and, indeed, insisted upon by these people. Now the ATP is forced to deal with success, if only by denial.

If you're doing the job by yourself, as so many have successfully done, learn to reward yourself. No one licks the alcohol problem without admirable effort. Notice that. Pat yourself on the back. Be pleased with your efforts.

The helper has to learn to insist that the recovering ATP recognize and be proud of his efforts, even if the ATP can't yet initiate such self-reward himself. In such cases the drinker must be made to face his or her characteristic denial of success; people can learn fairly readily to give themselves a passing grade for their own efforts. After a while they get sheepish if they don't.

The knack of self-reward is worth acquiring—it's quick, cheap, and honest rather than unrealistic. The self-helper *and* the helper of others need to develop the habit.

It is important, however, to distinguish between realistic self-reward and cockiness and overconfidence in someone who has made progress but is about to use it as an excuse to stop progressing. That, too, is a characteristic of some alcohol-damaged people, but contrary to widespread belief it is not universal among them. Rather than keeping all people recovering from alcohol troubles in a humble, "You've just started," self-distrusting state, we need to assess the individual's personality and ease him into the coping attitude *most helpful to him or her*. If you do not believe in yourself, learn to notice and capitalize on your accomplishments. There's no need to lie to yourself in this way more than any other.

Mistrusting the Geographical Cure

It's a good rule of thumb not to rely on the well-known and largely unsuccessful *geographical cure*, which means moving to another house, town, country, or job on the false premise that your alcohol troubles originate in something nearby. It is often helpful to work on the environment and the significant other people in it, but if you merely move, perhaps you'd better also plan to leave behind your head and all the memories and habits and coping mechanisms in it. If you drink when things go wrong, be assured that things go just as wrong in Boston as in San Francisco.

Assume that Joe Schlunk has many complaints about where and how he lives and relates that to his drinking. We transport him to a South Sea island, as per his request. He will soon discover, unless he is no longer Joe Schlunk, that the fountains in paradise are the wrong color, the perfumes too cloying, the weather too constantly lovely—and the beautiful native women he has been hankering for are all—lo!—brunettes and he likes blondes, and besides they seem after awhile to be too sexually demanding and he can't keep this up day after day. Poor lad. He's still Joe Schlunk.

Making Use of AA

As mentioned earlier, it is an excellent idea to think of Alcoholics Anonymous or one of the AA-oriented treatment programs in every instance. Many people find AA extraordinarily helpful both in attaining a life free of alcohol troubles and in sustaining it that way. Some people find AA enough, some need an additional, broader base, and others are actively turned off and driven away, but helper and helpee alike ought to try it. AA is available almost everywhere, or within a reasonable distance. On a trip to the Yucatan Peninsula in Mexico my wife and I were warmly greeted and royally squired about to meetings of an Al-Anon, Alateen, and two AA groups, and a friend who travels to Europe finds plenty of meetings there for himself. Another friend used to drink on business trips to the West Coast until he discovered AA and that it met out there, obviating the "need" for drinking at night out of "boredom."

I recommend as part of standard operating procedure that people unfamiliar with AA not decide against it too soon, because a lot of people who could use it sneak half-heartedly and embarrassed into one meeting, refuse to talk to members of the fellowship, and run away saying it's not for them. Each AA group has a different personality. In the beginning you may get turned on by one and off by another. Visit several, and say hello to people there—they want to help.

AA is in phone books and classified ads in the local newspaper. The police can help you find a meeting and so can the clergy or the local bartender. They meet nights, days, and weekends (mostly nights) so you cannot avoid on the basis of your work schedule.

AA has several kinds of meetings. The open meeting is for anyone who wants to make contact or learn about the fellowship, whether they have an alcohol problem or not. The closed meeting is for alcohol troubled people only. The stand-up meeting is one in which speakers tell their histories and how AA helped them, and those speakers are selected ahead of time, so you need not fear that you will be asked to talk. The discussion meeting is for people who want to participate in discussions rather than hear speeches.

AA also has a sponsorship program that has proved helpful to many. Under this system, if you hit it off with an individual, he or she may be willing to sponsor, guide, support, and advise you on a genuinely personal basis. People who form this arrangement, because of their special relationship, tend to become life-long friends.

If transportation is a problem, I don't believe AA members have ever refused to give people rides. In fact, they readily offer.

To reiterate, AA is suitable and helpful for a lot of people. It is not suitable and helpful for some others. Those others should keep trying another way, but only after taking an energetic look at AA and checking back once in a while. (You may well find that what was once not for you can later be extremely helpful.)

AA does *not* have all the answers, and it is *not* the last hope. As I have said, helping professionals (and I don't mean just alcohol-helping professionals) and family members in an alcohol troubled situation should take a good, open look at AA. It is the largest and most effective self-help group in the world, available to anyone anywhere without fee, and it utilizes group therapy techniques that could teach professionals some useful things.

A tip for the interested pro: When you do go, don't announce that you have no alcohol problem. See how you feel about being assumed to have an alcohol problem. Are you ashamed or embarrassed? You have a good value-testing opportunity—make the most of it to learn about yourself.

When the alcohol professional becomes adequately informed about AA, he or she will probably begin to refer routinely but should resist the temptation to which the untutored succumb—"dumping off" on AA rather than using the fellowship as a complementary, enriching maintenance system. The helper must not use AA to "wash his hands" of the problem. The ATP needs all the help he or she can get, and the professional should continue to provide it as long as it is useful.

Al-Anon, the self-help group which spun off AA to help spouses and family members of "alcoholics," should be mentioned prominently in a chapter on digging out of alcohol trouble. Al-Anon has been of inestimable value to myriads of unhappy, desperate spouses of "alcoholics"—usually but not always wives. Its cardinal principle, however, can cut two ways, one markedly positive, and the other nihilistic and counterproductive.

On the positive side, the basic principle is that one is in Al-Anon to help oneself, not the "alcoholic." This fundamental rule is extremely difficult for some people to fathom. Once comprehended, it can help remove resentment, unrealistic expectations, behavior on the part of the nondrinking spouse that the drinking partner has used for years to "excuse" continued drinking, and so forth. Al-Anon helps people understand that they are not to blame for the drinker's drinking, and that if they stay with the drinker they must adjust to the consequences of the drinking without destroying themselves. This understanding removes inappropriate guilt and, coupled with the support of fellow members, leads to substantial relief and often a freeing of feelings that allows more useful behavior than had been possible before.

On the negative side, however, Al-Anon's principle that one must help oneself sometimes gets misinterpreted as "One can't help the alcoholic." In consequence, too many spouses fail to take active steps to get additional help. Sometimes newcomers (whose husbands, let us say, are in minimal or moderate trouble) are advised very forcibly by the old-timers (whose husbands may be in severe and chronic alcohol trouble) not to try to help or intervene in the drinking process. What has for some Al-Anon members been so positive, then, can in some others appear to be advice to stop trying—too soon—to get help. These newcomers may find themselves yielding their good judgment to people whose claim to expertise is that their primary problem is not solved. The reasoning is similar to that of the president who appoints as secretary of defense in the new administration the very man who embroiled us in the last war—on the grounds that he is experienced.

A wife in Al-Anon against her husband's wishes (*he* was not an alcoholic, he claimed) heard elsewhere that she not only could learn to live with her husband's drinking but also could intervene in it, so she went to an alcohol helper. Shortly the husband came in. His alcohol intake, *exclusive* of what he imbibed outside the home, was a half gallon of gin every other day, dressed up in martinis. Initially, he did not see a problem, said he would not quit drinking, would not go to AA. He cut back to a half gallon twice a week.

We must agree that this was progress, but it was clearly not good enough, particularly when at the new rate he was beginning to refer to his drinking in the past tense ("When I used to drink").

The upshot, however, was that he gave up drinking completely. Al-Anon, while helpful in other ways, including to the wife under discussion, was nevertheless wrong on this one. The husband quit because of something she did.

In the process of gradually terminating the relationship with the alcohol helper, it developed that the wife's brother was married to an ATP who was going rapidly down the tube in an angrily dissolving marriage in a distant city. The wife, surprisingly, believed nothing could be done for the sister-in-law because "the alcoholic has to help herself." Her brother had tried (half-heartedly and ineffectually, it appeared to the helper) to get his wife to stop drinking. Eventually, however, when the wife was reminded that her efforts helped her husband, she motivated her brother to help his spouse—and the beginnings of that effort were, the last I heard, most encouraging.

Recognizing Positive Movement

The preceding story should help clarify the notion that often a spouse can begin the helping process and take part in it, rather than accepting blindly that a spouse "cannot help the alcoholic." In revealing that the husband in question proceeded from a half gallon of gin every other day through a half gallon twice a week to absolute and utter sobriety, I have also touched on a concept sometimes useful in digging out of trouble—the *Principle of Positive Movement.*

This principle depends on change—any change—in the desired direction. The desired goal is always to get the drinker into a nondrinking state. Anything closer to a nondrinking state shows positive movement. Surely, positive movement is *not the same* as a satisfactory outcome or conclusion, but it is a *partial success* and the helper should build on it. In the case of the man in the foregoing story, a start was made in the desired direction because (1) there seemed no way to get him to quit immediately and completely; (2) he refused to go to AA; and (3) to cut down his alcohol intake afforded him partial success (which he doubted he could achieve) and cleared up his chemically burdened brain a little so that it could receive messages better in the next round of attempts to get him to stop.

Some AA people frown on and make fun of anything like the principle of positive change. They feel that one is either drinking or not drinking and that there are no half-way measures. So do I, unless I can't get the ideal, and then I'll settle for what I can get at the moment—and build on it. I'll try to help someone achieve sobriety for a month if I can, or a week, or a couple of days, or a day at a time. If a man hasn't drawn a sober breath for years and then drinks nothing for four days—and then drinks again—at least notice that the four days is positive movement. Or if a woman has drunk a fifth of scotch a day and shifts to a six-pack of beer on Saturday night, it is clearly not accurate to say she's out of trouble, but hasn't she begun to come to grips with some issues? Aren't we pretty sure she can hear us better?

Learning About Medication

In digging out, or helping others dig out of trouble, *learn something about medication.* Alcohol-involved persons, as noted before, tend to be addictive and chemical-oriented and are at ultra high risk for abusing medications. In addition, medications are in extremely wide use today, with a rainbow-colored cornucopia in many a bathroom medicine cabinet.

Be alert to all mind-benders and mood-changers, among which are some tranquilizers, all barbiturates, many painkillers, many "sleepers," all amphetamines. As discussed in Chapter 5, Valium is dangerous to alcohol-prone persons, and I keep hearing that Librium is, although personally I do not yet see that as a problem except in severe stages. Phenobarbital is bad because it, like other barbiturates, tends to get used in combination with alcohol and people often die with that intoxicating, addicting combination. The painkiller Percodan is easily misused, as is the hospital liquid sleeper, chloral hydrate. Cough medicines may have codeine or alcohol in them. And so forth.

As mentioned earlier, AA people have been so opposed to medication that they have sometimes removed medications the actively drinking individual needs to stay alive or to stay well, such as high blood pressure medication, anticoagulants, diabetes medication, digitalis, and anticonvulsants. The alcohol-damaged person should steer clear of the energizers like Dexedrine, or *any* amphetamine. Prescribers of medication must become more alert to these implications and attempt to learn better systems for identifying alcohol-jeopardized people before prescribing, and primary persons or their families need to ask the prescribing physician what the drug is, and in the last analysis must defend against the prescribing action of the uninformed physician.

Antabuse, on the other hand, is a pill that can be useful. Taken each morning, it provides protection against compulsive drinking since it produces a nauseating, often dangerous reaction to the ingestion of alcohol for two to five days. It should *not* be prescribed for someone not completely off alcohol. Antabuse has no apparent ill effect if not mixed with alcohol, but it should be remembered that alcohol is contained in some substances we don't think about in connection with alcohol troubles—cough medicine, for example. Antabuse should be prescribed only after discussion with the primary person as to its effects and should not be given to people who may take it without regard to (or maybe because of) the dangerous, potentially fatal, reaction if taken with alcohol. Nor should it be employed as a lifelong solution—the reasoned decision to not drink must become one's protection.

Anticonvulsants like Dilantin and Mysoline should not be withdrawn without discussion with the prescribing physician. Some tranquilizers are useful for a time, although generally the ATP eventually must learn to deal with life without chemicals, and sometimes that should be done sooner rather than later.

The antidepressant medications, such as Elavil and Tofranil, will prove a major boon to ATPs. They are not basically dangerous to alcohol-damaged people as far as we can now determine. They do not produce a high in most people, but in hefty dosages they may produce some dizziness, which suggests that we should keep an eye on them. Lithium carbonate so far seems safe in this regard for cyclical, up-and-down mood swings, or for the highs or lows alone.

Act as if alcohol-impaired people are honest-to-god people. They may be sick or crazy for a time, or they may sometimes appear to be dishonest, but you will quickly find that they are entitled to and thrive under courtesy, warmth, honesty (including either a kick in the ass or praise), and in general a fair shake.

Not *"all alcoholics are liars."* One first learns not to believe too readily, and then learns to ask better questions and to make better observations. If you ask "set-up" questions designed to back people into corners, you'll get a lot of untruths, but recall that you have the power to produce that kind of behavior by your attitude. While perhaps you needn't believe too quickly, neither must you automatically disbelieve. Hold your belief versus disbelief in limbo. There's no hurry, and many alcohol-impaired people will be as straight as an arrow; others will be as honest as they can be at the moment; some will be responding at the moment to the side of their ambivalence that says "I'll quit"; a few will have a code of honor that will not permit them to lie in the face of the right question; and so forth, with many possibilities of truths, half truths, untruths, and just plain confusion.

A *dry drunk* is an episode of extreme anxiety, often accompanied by the shakes, in someone who drank heavily at one time but who is now sober and has been for as long as eighteen months or two years. The experience is called a dry drunk because it feels as if one is coming off a bender and that a drink will settle everything back into shape just the way it used to. The dry drunk episode is not common, but when it happens one must put a label on it quickly; people in the throes of this desperate state are strongly tempted to drink again—"I didn't feel this bad when I was drinking. What the hell is happening to me, anyway?"

Call it by its name, quickly. Labeling has a potent relieving effect, since it places the dry drunk episode in the known and understood category. Tell the individual (or remind yourself if you're having it) that it is self-limiting and will be gone in ten days or sooner. This is no time for the helper to shilly-shally. Give it the name quickly, and then support the individual in any way you can—by making frequent calls or visits, or by alerting the family or employer. The dry drunk is experienced as fairly pure anxiety and is almost certainly physiological, occurring during the time in which the body, particularly the brain, readjusts to functioning in a nonalcohol chemical bath. Here again, give attention to the success—one cannot have a dry drunk unless one was a heavy drinker who carried off a remarkably persistent and successful effort at sobriety. Congratulations are realistically in order, and it would surely help to offer them.

Frequent, brief helping contacts are generally measurably superior for the alcohol struggler than, say, an hour or four hours once a week. This fact is a blessing in a way because the helper doesn't get worn out so fast as he would with the intensive, energy-sapping kinds of contacts mental health helpers are prone to deliver. People with moderate and severe cases of alcohol damage have short memories and enjoy and benefit from frequent greetings and from short, pithy, straight-line, no-nonsense involvement. They can be made uncomfortable by the development of an intensive personal relationship and may use long contacts to justify themselves, to lead you astray, or in some other unprofitable fashion. They need time between "wisdom-deliveries" to think and absorb, and they have short attention spans.

Two twenty-minute sessions on, say, Monday and Thursday are infinitely more productive than one big deal of an hour and a half during the week. Inpatient or residential settings can and should deliver several or many helping and social contacts per day.

Like all rules, this one on brevity can be broken if you feel it should be. One day I came home absolutely exhausted by a session with a husband (in alcohol trouble) and a wife (more interested in blaming him for being an inadequate husband than in helping him to solve his problems so he could be an adequate one). Both were strong personalities. Since he was hospitalized and in severe immediate alcohol difficulties and I didn't know when I could get to talk with her again, I stayed with them for perhaps three hours. We made excellent progress, but I ended up absolutely drained, and when I dragged into the house my wife asked me what was the matter. I told her I felt like a marshmallow that had been in a field with two rampaging steamrollers.

So once in a while one can profitably spend blocks of time on problems. Incidentally, in your efforts to go in a straight line on the alcohol issues and to say things in ways that can be heard, *you cannot expect to be well liked all the time*. In the foregoing instance I was not liked at all for some time, but the final upshot was that the husband went back to work as a CPA and my wife and I have been guests at the wife's excellent restaurant on several occasions. When we walk in, she calls her husband up and he comes to the restaurant to say hello and to socialize.

Learning About Available Facilities

Many residential treatment programs are available across the country, and I would be gravely remiss not to discuss them, since in some situations they can be tremendously useful in getting underway. Current philosophy and practice determine that most individuals who submit themselves to residential care for alcohol problems are in severe trouble as measured by the definitional criteria I have presented. An apparently increasing number of people in moderate trouble also avail themselves of these services, which is an encouraging trend, and yet even then they tend to be drawn from the most damaged end of the moderate category.

Many facilities still exist solely or primarily for detoxification, or "detox," a process that does little more than dry people out, withdraw them from alcohol, over a three- to ten-day period. Such facilities, while needed, are grossly deficient in reeducational facilities, since it is not usually possible to provide substantive rehabilitative or reeducational services in three to ten days.

"Dry-out farms" have existed for years, often in pastoral settings, and are usually devoted to the quick withdrawal from alcohol of people who can pay. They are typically short on professional personnel, follow-up, broad-scale reeducation, and an ability and interest in sweeping members of the family unit into the process. On discharge they generally refer primarily or only to AA, if to any follow-up system. Dry-out farms have been basically unidimensional in attempting to solve what we know to be a multidimensional problem.

Those who cannot pay are typically detoxified, if at all, in large city hospitals with units catering to severe alcohol problems en masse, in state institutions, and in social service agency flophouses. Some "drunk tanks"—the lockups in city police stations for inebriates and physically impaired alcohol-damaged people alike—have remarkably hu-

mane systems and personnel. Others, of course, are abomi-
nations. Almost all are hit-or-miss operations that keep
people locked up to "sleep it off" unless they start to bleed,
convulse, or go into DTs, at which point they are transferred
to the hospital for the shortest possible time. In recent years
"alcoholism" has been decriminalized, meaning simply that
by legal decree it is no longer a crime to have an alcohol
problem and authorities are charged with treating rather
than incarcerating the alcohol-impaired individual. Since
decriminalization, "Hospital" signs have appeared in some
big city drunk tanks—with no alteration whatever except
the addition of the signs.

All these systems serve a minimal purpose, and I would
not wish to see them dismantled until better systems replace
them. They do keep many people alive long enough to get
squared away later, and that is worthwhile. Too many
people die unnecessarily, however, and the system produces
the "revolving door" syndrome. In my state detoxification
facility, which serves about 1,500 admissions per year, about
300 individuals are served annually, and almost none receives reeducation. Although the facility is inefficient and
unimaginative—and frighteningly expensive for such low-
quality care—my community includes many sober, well
adjusted older people who went through the process.

Most people still withdraw at home, unsupported medically. Many can do so very safely because they are not
severe or chronic cases, which are the principal grist for
the revolving-door mills, but have instead moderate or
minimal degrees of involvement.

Again, persons in danger of DTs and those with other
serious medical problems should be detoxified only where
there is ready access to medical support. I am fully aware
of the burgeoning industry of nonmedical detox facilities
that claim, and I believe have, very few serious medical
complications. Such facilities are, or should be, staffed by
knowledgeable people who know when to call for medical
help.

Detox thus can be used as a short-term stop-gap, but such a system avoids long-term issues and thus contributes to society's disillusionment and pessimism. (You treat them inadequately for the long haul and then use the inadequate outcomes to maintain that you'd be unsuccessful if you did it properly.) Detox can be used very profitably as the first step in a treatment and reeducation system.

Vastly superior would be to have enough general hospitals with alcohol-wise personnel to perform the relatively short-term detox function and then transfer people to longer-term residential facilities. Such a system would represent the most efficient, safest, and productive use of manpower and buildings, and would also serve the important function of alerting and training all hospital personnel to the nature of alcohol problems, which now drift silently and largely undiagnosed onto general medical, surgical, and psychiatric units. In short, we would get double mileage—skilled and safe professional services plus education of the health community.

Criteria for Quality Facilities

Suppose we had a sufficient number of quality detox facilities, whether of the hospital model or the nonmedical (but skilled) one. The development of a sufficient quantity of good quality detox and diagnostic facilities is well on its way and is *relatively* easy compared to the even more desirable establishment of programs and facilities devoted to decreasing the incidence of the alcohol problem over the long haul.

To what sort of facility would we wish to refer after detoxification? What kinds of problems might respond best to residential treatment or, as I prefer to think of it, reeducation?

Our discussion must branch here onto two different tracks, one dealing with some of the issues regarding facilities and services themselves, and the other concerned with the kinds of individuals who ought to benefit most from them.

The ideal facility does not exist widely at the present time. It would have broad scope and a capability for grappling with, and solving, a wide range of problems. Throughout, however, it would have to retain the capacity for a straight-line approach directed unswervingly toward alcohol troubles. Private facilities will in the nature of things set the standards, but public programs can, in fact, be not far behind and can even lead the way in some respects.

Good residential programs concern themselves with the following: they insist on quality care; they are concerned with the *relevant* aspects of physical facilities; they select staff carefully; they involve the family; they emphasize education and training; and they provide for a reasonable return rate.

Quality Care

The phrase "quality care" must be stated, believed, restated, and adhered to. Quality care requires, in the last analysis, the setting of professional standards and principles and adhering to them through thick and thin. I have indicated elsewhere that principles (and, here, standards) are of diluted and diminished value if applied only when it is comfortable to apply them. Rather, they should be applied when they are useful, *especially* when the going gets rough. If the standards are well thought out originally, and are therefore good ones, they will usually be helpful.

A physician was referred to a residential treatment facility that had proved its worth with ATPs of modest social and economic status. He was severely alcohol-impaired, very bright, verbal, and persuasive. He had also made a career (a checkered one) of using his title, "Doctor," to impress people. The facility had a rule, and a quite proper one, that residents not have the use of their automobiles. Within four days this man had use of his automobile, was given leave to attend to his affairs (which could have been done in several other ways) and, predictably, ended up bolting from the place less dry than when he arrived, which wasn't dry at all. That is not quality care, and nobody derived any benefit from this particular incident.

The standards were sound, but in failing to uphold them the management both cheated and jeopardized the client. To deliver quality care you develop sound guidelines and stick to them because they embody valid principles, not because they're easy. The principles are constructed in the first place to ensure the best possible outcome, and they can be violated *only for that reason*, and certainly not solely for someone's comfort. Standards can be somewhat different from place to place depending on treatment philosophy, but they must be high, consistent, *and valued enough to be followed*.

Relevant Aspects of Physical Facilities

There is a rumor abroad that a homelike atmosphere, the little cottage with the white picket fence, somehow contributes to the therapeutic or reeducation enterprise. No hard data support this belief, although it is widely trumpeted about in the field. Nor do the facilities need to be fancy, unless the absence of amenities would make it psychologically impossible for specific people to remain in the reeducation setting.

I would trade "homey" for "fireproof" any day. An easy maintenance structure is infinitely preferable to a large, hard-to-clean facility that requires the engagement of cleaning and maintenance personnel rather than helpers and their services. The physical arrangements, ideally, will provide space that can be utilized for seminars, group meetings, and AA sessions. There will be facilities for quiet time, so individuals thinking seriously about their problems and the directions their lives are taking can do so. There should be areas for small-group socializing and talking about personal issues, since people in trouble are extremely effective in helping other people in trouble. There should be psychologically and physically comfortable locations for private, one-to-one counseling and dialogues. Clients should probably not be in single bedrooms except under unusual circumstances, since people in trouble have a real need to learn to resocialize and relate to other people.

Staff and Philosophy

Staff is critical, and sufficent staff is obviously required. Given a solid core of regular full-time people, it is probably best to maintain a consulting list of skilled and experienced persons who can deliver specific and sometimes specialized services as needed. In this category might be, for example, a neurologist, an expert in group therapy or group process, somebody excellent at engaging the individual in the early phases of reeducation, somebody good with families, at finances, and so forth. Above all, such helpers need to be honest, direct, and better off than the client in the areas in which they are helping.

A good facility should have a *mix* of (1) trained professionals who can "go at least two ways"—the psychologist must know alcohol as well as psychology—and (2) people who, while perhaps not trained in a specific professional discipline, have helpful personalities and solid experience in alcohol troubles. The mix of nonprofessional and professional is required for several reasons, the most important of which is that operations without the mix, or with an unbalanced ratio, simply do not work as well as those that solicit and desire the open-mindedness that comes with a diversity of skills and outlooks.

The best quality services are delivered by staffs and facilities balanced and coordinated for the purpose of offering a reasoned, consistent, *total* package to the client. The total experience is developed out of a reservoir of varied and disparate skills, experiences, and personalities.

For these reasons a good facility needs a proper mix or balance between staff who have had alcohol problems and those who have not. It is only a partial, not a total, recommendation that an individual at one time could not relate wisely to alcohol and has now overcome the problem. The staff should include some persons with the credibility provided by prior alcohol troubles; but a quality treatment program also needs to have personnel whose outlook, personalities, and learning experiences prevented them from ever having alcohol problems. An all-non-AA staff is as limited and narrow in outlook as an all-AA staff.

Families and Significant Others

A great weakness in current alcohol circles and treatment facilities is that important other people in the ATP's life are often left out of the reeducation process. This is particularly wasteful and tragic since many of these people (employers, spouses, children, co-workers) are bright, eager to help, and *very* effective when pointed in the right direction. They also have a great deal to gain personally if the damaged person improves. Many significant others accompany ATPs to facilities primarily to see that they get there, to sign the papers, to take away the valuables, and to go away as quickly as possible.

Under such circumstances, the ATP spends four to ten weeks in an intensive relearning experience and returns to an interpersonal situation that is unchanged and uncomprehending of the major new changes in him. The significant others, through no fault of their own, are left unable to be of informed assistance day by day when the helpee returns to his ordinary environment, replete with its old stresses, habit systems, reminders, and temptations.

This is not to say that one cannot dig out of troubles

on one's own, or even, sadly, in the face of screwed-up significant others blockading one's good intentions, because
of course thousands of people do so. In the last analysis,
if it's *your* belly or *your* sunny days that are destroyed by
booze, then it's *your* trouble and *you'll* have to handle it
come hell or high water, even though it's easier and more
often successful if you have willing and informed helpers
near at hand.

It is reasonable, though, for helpers to attempt to educate and inform and recruit into the treatment system a
supportive network of significant, caring family members.
The wife often does not know where to turn or what to do.
As she becomes informed she can question the use of Valium
with her ATP husband. She can go to Al-Anon. Rather than
unrealistically suggest that the husband go to AA cold, she
can attend a few meetings and then help him get there after
she knows where it is, who might speak personally with her
husband, whether it is a group suited for him, and so forth.

The university with which I am associated has developed a peer counseling system in the Health Educator's
office. Undergraduate students, initially recruited and informed in an alcohol class, undergo further training and
disperse into dormitories, the student union, and the student newspaper, deal with campus police, with administrators, with the student infirmary staff, and so on. Their enthusiasm and creativity are extremely high. They produce
alcohol awareness fairs, sponsor an educational group for
fellow students and their parents, and address staff from
other colleges and universities regarding our system.

Fanning out as they do into what amounts to a city
of 10,000, they have been remarkably effective in helping
fellow students with alcohol problems. Useful as this has
been, however, it has become clear that the student alcohol
team is potentially of the greatest help in counseling and
informing students regarding what to do about alcohol
troubles in their parents. We are beginning to think of the
members of the team not only as community educators,

which they most definitely are, but as "catchers" of people in trouble with alcohol—very often in family members. Although we are on the East Coast, one student is learning to mobilize her family network in Louisiana to help an ATP parent; a young man with two ATP parents in California is also building a helping network via mail and telephone calls and visits, with the aid of younger siblings living with the parents.

We are convinced that family support systems can and must be constructed in order to maximize benefits. A major part of this effort revolves first around informing the family member who becomes the primary intervener, and then helping that individual mobilize and inform the rest of the family so that the ATP faces a common, informed front.

Education and Training

Quality alcohol facilities should be oriented toward education and training, because techniques and systems learned in the front lines are often different from those developed in the laboratories and think tanks. The quality facility continues to seek better ways. Once the better ways are learned, they are tested and taught to others. Better ways are never found by people who already have the only best way.

I would like to persuade helpers to use terms like "education" or "reeducation" rather than "rehabilitation," since rehabilitation is used when referring to physically ill and severely handicapped persons. In keeping with one of the major themes of this book, it may perhaps be used validly with severely damaged individuals but not with the vast majority of people in alcohol trouble.

The term "rehabilitation" also presupposes the prior existence of an adult life that did not rely substantially on chemical coping mechanisms, and many people in alcohol trouble never did develop strong and reliable systems without drugs or alcohol. The beauty, then, of being in trouble with alcohol and then getting out of it is that one has an opportunity to uncover, in several important life areas, far better abilities than one ever had. It's hard for people in trouble to know that at the time, but it's true nevertheless.

The process of giving up alcohol is appropriately called educational because it is, first, an unlearning of old habits, and then a relearning of more profitable and growth-producing ones; this reeducation occurs in a setting of ever-lessening anxiety, tension, and fear.

Return Rate

The quality facility will build in provisions for an appropriate return rate. Some ATPs will falter or slip for a time; they must feel comfortable about returning to the facility without experiencing crippling shame, and they must be able to return to a genuinely welcoming environment when they need to and not feel impelled to stay away because they are temporary "failures."

For some people, in some situations, getting out of alcohol trouble is a long and progressive journey, not a one-shot deal (although, as I have noted several times, there are many, many rapid and at the same time lasting comebacks). The person with chronic and severe impairment may well require a three- to five-year trip back. Families or other emotionally significant supporting people have to be recontacted and a mutually satisfactory relationship rebuilt. Bodies have to be brought back to health, or, if damaged beyond the point where complete recovery is possible, the ATP must adjust to the impairment. Checkered employment histories have to be repaired. Emotions and new coping skills need to be tried and practiced. Learning to bear an unaccustomed, slightly higher level of anxiety takes awhile, and that learning can best occur when the individual is getting the payoff of success in some areas.

The old friends, helpers and helpees, should have a comfortable way of coming together again should the urge or need arise, or even if it looks as if it is going to arise. Returning to recharge the batteries a bit now and then must not be regarded as a failure. New problem-solving, life-coping skills take at least as much practice and coaching as learning to play tennis or to swim.

Many persuasive reasons exist for undertaking residential treatment, among which are rapidity of learning, getting people under cover and away from stress, preventing them from destroying deteriorating family or employment relationships while their judgment is clouded and behavior inappropriate, and so forth. It may be that trying to make progress on the outside has been unsuccessful.

Reasons for *not* electing residential assistance may be financial or may be related to a shaky employment situation that might be irretrievably damaged or lost by, say, three weeks' absence. On the other hand, often the employer can be persuaded by a representative of the residential facility to be an ally and helper of his employee when the latter finally makes a potentially useful and open decision to seek such help. Increasingly, employers are willing to listen to a straightforward pitch that may lead to salvaging a valuable worker. Large companies, in fact, sometimes even pay for the residential experience. Business and industry also are learning to make continued employment contingent on getting help. It's a threat, but it's also a fact of life.

If a given community has strong outpatient or nonresidential resources and no good inpatient ones, that fact might also dictate a choice to work on the problems at home. The two best reasons for not going to a residential setting may or may not be related—the first is that the individual did not really need it, and the second is that if people can bite the bullet they may have a subsequent feeling of pride and renewed self-esteem if they can carry it off on the outside.

Often the decision to go to a short-term detox setting is made by others and forced on the primary person by the facts—a withdrawal situation and/or a need to get "under cover." These, I stress, are severe cases and should always, at least ideally, be followed by longer-term systematic re-education. The longer-term, residential enterprise often is less of an immediate emergency but may well be the most economical choice.

Many people who would benefit greatly from residence in a facility do *not* need detoxification but clearly need to be isolated from a deteriorating situation in order to get on their feet, to come to a decision to attack their alcohol problems, and to acquire the resources and personal skills to be successful.

I cannot overemphasize that in cases of doubt as to whether or not significant alcohol troubles exist it is far more efficient to get an early opinion, and the quality facility can be of marked assistance in diagnosis. We must leave room in the quality residential facility for admission of people in doubt, not only of far-gone or severe cases. It is completely legitimate to elect a treatment or reeducation residential facility to obtain expert assistance in diagnosis before deciding to do something about the troubles, and as part of making an actual start on them. These places, when competent, can be superbly helpful in this regard.

Remember that the modal length of stay in a detoxification facility is under ten days, and often as short as three, and that *three weeks* seems to be the minimum for a reeducation facility. People do not get the "cobwebs" or the "cement" out of their heads soon enough to make two weeks seem a substantial or useful investment.

Specific Suggestions

Hundreds of helpful methods and techniques have been devised by those who have been working in the area of alcohol troubles, whether as helpers or helpees. Because we know there is no such thing as *a* cause, or *a* given personality, or *one* life circumstance that leads to difficulties in relating to alcohol, it is important always to keep in mind the general principles discussed in this book to cover attitudes and understandings of the problems. To these generalities must be added the specific method or methods that will help.

Mostly for the helper—*reduce anxiety* (not life's realistic pressures) *wherever you can,* to reduce the strength of the S or stimulus of anxiety in the S-R paradigm. That may involve assuming a directorial or even a benevolently dictatorial role for a while. It may involve calling an employer, or being positive and optimistic (but only if that is honest), or doing anything else that will reduce tension *realistically.*

If the ATP is carrying a hundred-pound sack of emotional tension on her shoulders and you can get six pounds of it off this week by talking to her child's teacher, do so. Reducing anxiety so that flexibility of response is increased, and paying off nondrinking coping is the business you are in. Do not be lured away from the alcohol issue either by the helpee's funny little mind or by your desire to reduce anxiety. Again, you cannot deviate from the straight line, even though you don't have to verbalize about it all the time. You must hold your purpose in your own mind, at least.

A system used very successfully by some of the old-timers is called *"passing the thought."* This simple stratagem requires only that when the urge to drink strikes, you put it away for just the moment, by a conscious act of will. One merely passes it through and out of the mind, replacing it with another. Passing the thought is either a first cousin or a parent of AA's famous "Day at a Time," which has been of help to hundreds of thousands of people. AA people say, "I'm not going to worry about whether or not I'll drink tomorrow. I'll get through *today* without taking a drink."

Some people, mostly those in the minimal and moderate categories, are fortunate enough to be able to stop drinking without feeling almost overwhelming urges to drink. We have learned to be wary of persons who believe they are out of difficulty because they haven't had an urge for a week or two, and I have learned to share my wariness with them: "I'd be more sure of your progress if you had

had an urge and beaten it down." Occasionally it might help to adopt the following practical system, which may or may not have a scientific basis but which seems to work clinically and is sometimes very helpful to the person in the grip of repeated, recurring urges to drink:

Inside every person who has powerful, often sudden urges to drink there is a limited number of such episodes. We do not know how many of these are sprinkled in your future, but it may help you to know that each time you feel one of them, face it, and actively refrain from drinking, you will have erased it from your bag of future episodes. On the other hand, every time you drink when an urge hits you, you build a future urge that will have to be faced later. Therefore, every urge that *is* resisted represents a real success and real progress in the future as well as at the moment. Thus, you can win twice—now and later.

Conclusion

It would seem abundantly clear that we as a nation or society are not deliberately and consciously refusing to face issues and problems in the alcohol area and thereby purposely consigning many ATPs among us to readily avoidable miseries and pain. Presumably we are beginning to perceive the negative results of broad-scale misunderstandings, misinformation, and misattributions in the alcohol field. That most ATPs are not addicted to alcohol, for example, can become evident to the most casual observer making an informed observation.

We need now to conduct critical, analytical reevaluations of our old beliefs. Taking action, or digging out of trouble, cannot be perceived as a task only for individuals if we agree that society has difficulty grappling with the problems. In this connection I must debunk one more myth, which for the sake of consistency with Chapter 2 I will label Myth V.

Myth V is that the way to reduce alcohol problems in

the society at large is to increase the number of alcohol programs, specialized units in hospitals, courts, mental health clinics, and so on, and to increase the number of trained alcohol counselors. A corollary of Myth V is that an increased number of tagged or alcohol specialty dollars will necessarily lead to an increase in the number and scope of good programs.

We must grant, I think, that the massive infusion of funds, particularly federal funds, into the alcohol area, principally through NIAAA, has increased alcohol awareness. Perhaps that was necessary for a time, although a strong case could be made that much of that effort will eventually have to be undone; many of the staff and programs that resulted are based on the old misinformation, uncritically accepted and only partially learned. Huge numbers of people who are now heading up programs or counseling ATPs have had *no* training whatever. It can be contended that they hurt the movement and give it a bad name and that as a result funding will eventually be withdrawn.

Even if we grant that the maxi-bucks were at one time helpful, it appears that we must now begin to consider Phase II, the coordination and integration of alcohol efforts into the health delivery and health education systems—in both health and mental health areas. Alcohol efforts, where they exist, are now largely additions or excrescences on other programs.

We are certain, for example, that about 50 percent of adults who come to mental health operations for help have some substantial and significant alcohol-associated disorder, such as depression, anxiety, marital discord, irritability, delusional perceptions, poor reality testing, and so forth. The same is true of health operations, as discussed earlier.

To insert alcohol counselors or alcohol specialty units into (or onto, as an excrescence) ongoing systems is to remove from the staffs of the existing systems the responsibility that is properly theirs—to identify and treat, as early as possible, the whole person, including the alcohol involve-

ment, and to engage in preventive and educational efforts.
The mere existence of an alcohol specialist or specialty unit
obviates the necessity for the helper who works as an in-
tegral part of a mental health clinic or a hospital emergency
room, for example, to learn about identification, prevention,
and the like. As a result, they can refer only severe, chronic,
or otherwise obvious alcohol problems to the expert.

If around 50 percent of adults who go to mental health
clinics have a significant alcohol involvement, and if the
same is true for adult beds in general medical and surgical
hospitals, it appears only logical that *all* helpers in such
identification and treatment settings must acquire alcohol-
related skills; there should be, at the very least, a standard,
minimal level of information.

Look at it this way—should it be standard operating
procedure for all personnel in the hospital emergency room
to learn to take temperatures, or does it make better sense
to appoint an expensive "fever team" to come down to take
temperatures *only* on patients who the untrained emergency
room personnel think may have a fever? (In addition, we
already know that one of every two patients in the emergency room may have a fever and that the skills and attitudes necessary to take temperatures are relatively easily
acquired.)

The very act of creating a "fever team" under those
circumstances will lead quite naturally to a failure on the
part of other personnel to learn the rudiments of fever identification, just as the construction of an alcohol specialty
team can let other personnel off the hook with regard to
learning the rudiments of alcohol troubles.

It may well be that persons with identified fevers
should, *after diagnosis,* be referred to the proper treatment
setting, just as we call the orthopedist when the emergency
room personnel diagnose a possible broken bone. But we do
not typically staff the emergency room with an entire regi-
ment of specialists—we expect tentative diagnoses to be
made by trained personnel, and *then* the obstetrical, pedi-

atric, surgical, neurological, and other specialists are called in.

The alcohol specialist problem can be regarded in still another way. Can we logically expect that as we place in the field increasing numbers of alcohol counselors (many of whom, as we have seen, are inadequately or not at all trained), they will substantially ameliorate the alcohol problems in the population at large? Certainly not if their presence relieves the average health provider of the responsibility to learn the rudiments of the alcohol problem area. Certainly not if they are given the label and tasks of "alcohol counselors"—they will essentially work with already identified "alcoholics" or ATPs. While that is a worthy goal, it does not even *address* some important issues.

A small county in my state has approximately 100,000 people. Estimates of the incidence of "alcoholism" (which usually signifies the severe and obvious) range between about 2 and 10 percent. Thus, the county under discussion is estimated to have between 2,000 and 10,000 "alcoholics." Suppose an alcohol counselor can carry a caseload (not identify, not educate, not prevent, but only treat) of 100 "alcoholics." The number of alcohol counselors required to treat this little rural county's ATPs would range between 20 and 100. Assume that to hire, administer, support with secretarial help, provide phones and transportation for, pay Blue Cross and sick leave and vacations for, one counselor costs $10,000 per year. Thus, in this little county we are estimating $200,000 to $1 million per year to treat the already damaged "alcoholic."

In the meantime we have two county hospitals, a community mental health clinic, a university counseling service, countless physicians, psychiatrists, and other mental health personnel, clergy, school counselors, and the like. *None* of these resources receives, or sees the need to receive, formal or substantial training in "taking temperatures" for alcohol problems.

The point is that we should consider the *negative* as

well as the positive effects in tooling up new alcohol counselor programs. In my opinion, there should be no such thing as an alcohol counselor. That concept and job description should be replaced with "alcohol educator-counselor" or some such title, and a job description directing the incumbent to educate and mobilize the entire help-providing community. We have resources—we need to educate and train them. We must integrate and embed alcohol knowledge into the health and mental health systems. To do less is to construct a predictably doomed or ineffectual system.

I sit on a commission that passes on the doling out of alcohol grant money, and I have learned that health providers believe they cannot be expected to provide quality care (here related to the care of the individual whose basic problems—undiagnosed alcohol troubles—mask as other health problems) unless they are specifically funded to do so. I submit that mental health and health care providers, by failing to inform themselves regarding the 50 percent of their clients who are ATPs, are in fact *not* providing minimal quality care. Our commission deals with the grant applications of agency after agency that says in essence, "We cannot provide services to 'alcoholics' unless we are provided with additional alcohol-tagged dollars."

They are dealing with ATPs now and don't know it. Why should it cost more money to treat people for what ails them, a point which at least raises the possibility that the treatment could be more cost-effective?

The health and mental health sectors frequently do not send representatives to workshops, courses, and symposia on the subject—even though the programs cost them nothing whatever. I submit that by providing such uninformed agencies with money for alcohol counselors we run serious risks of actually paying to compound the difficulties discussed here—buying "fever teams" rather than requiring all personnel to know the basics of their trade.

I began this chapter by introducing you to the demon

Screwtape. It seems fitting that he should have the last but one comment in the book:

"An ever increasing craving for an ever diminishing pleasure is the formula. It is more certain; and it's better *style* to get the man's soul and give him *nothing* in return—that is what really gladdens [the Devil's] heart.

"As always, the first step is to keep knowledge out of his mind. Do not let him suspect the law of undulation. Let him assume that the first ardours of his conversion might have been expected to last, and ought to have lasted, forever, and that his present dryness is an equally permanent condition. Having once got this misconception well fixed in his head, you may then proceed in various ways. It all depends on whether your man is of the desponding type who can be tempted to despair, or of the wishful-thinking type who can be assured that all is well."

You have a good start and a hopeful outlook, be you a primary person or a helper. Screwtape and his tribe are clever and ingenious but usually manage to lose. Sooner is better than later, so you should start now. Try everything that could work, and be persistent.

I believe you will have success in your venture and wish you well and warmly.

Index

237